THE IDAHO CONVERSION KIT

How to be an Idahoan in Ten Easy Steps

THE IDAHO CONVERSION KIT

How to be an Idahoan in Ten Easy Steps

RICK JUST

The Idaho Conversion Kit: How to be an Idahoan in Ten Easy Steps
Copyright © 2023 by Rick Just

All rights reserved. No part of this book may be reproduced or transmitted in any form or by any means, electronic or mechanical, including photocopying, recording, or by any information storage and retrieval system, without written permission from Cedar Creek Press, LLC. Brief quotes for the purpose of reviews are allowed.

Book design, typography, and photo work by Meggan Laxalt Mackey, Studio M Publications and Design LLC, Boise, Idaho.

Edited by Stacey Smekofske.

Library of Congress Cataloging-in-Publication Data
Just, Rick, 1949—.
    The Idaho Conversion Kit: How to be an Idahoan in Ten Easy Steps

Summary: How to be an Idahoan in Ten Easy Steps. Or, one easy step. Get yourself born here. You're home-free if you were smart enough to be born in Idaho. You can slap an Idaho Native bumper sticker on your Prius right now and skip the rest of the book. But, if you can't check off a high percentage of the following steps, you'll fit in like a duck in Oxfords. *You're technically an Idahoan, but are you a **real** Idahoan?*

Other Books by Rick Just
Anjel
The Wizards Trilogy: Wizard Girl, Wizard Chase, Wizard's End
Ghost Writer
100 Years: Idaho and Its Parks
Idaho Snapshots
Idaho's State Parks (Images of America)
Keeping Private Idaho
A Kid's Guide to Boise
Fearless: The Story of Farris Lind, the Man Behind the Skunk
Speaking of Idaho History Series No 1: Symbols, Signs and Songs

Published by **CEDAR CREEK PRESS, LLC**
BOISE, IDAHO

ISBN 978-1-7341924-5-2
FIRST PRINTING UNITED STATES OF AMERICA

DEDICATION

In Memory of Merle Wells
Idaho's Most Knowledgeable Non-native

CONTENTS

HOW TO BE AN IDAHOAN IN TEN EASY STEPS

1 Idaho Place Names 5

2 The Shape of Idaho 5

3 Idaho License Plates 5

4 Idaho Symbols 5

5 Idaho Superlatives 5

6 Lake Monsters 5

7 Nicknames 5

8 The Jockey Box 5

9 The Gem State 5

10 Famous Connections 5

HOW TO BE AN IDAHOAN IN TEN EASY STEPS

Or, in one easy step. Get yourself born here. You're home-free if you were smart enough to be born in Idaho. You can slap an Idaho Native bumper sticker on your Prius right now and skip the rest of the book. But, if you can't check off a high percentage of the following steps, you'll fit in like a duck in Oxfords. *You're technically an Idahoan, but are you a **real** Idahoan?*

1. Learn how to pronounce Idaho place names.
Practice saying Boise without using a Z.

2. Learn to distinguish Idaho from every other state simply by shape.

3. Be able to tell where drivers are from *just by looking at their license plates!*

4. Know all the Idaho state symbols.

5. Know one Idaho superlative for every finger on your right hand.

6. Remember the names of Idaho's two major lake monsters.

7. Know the story of at least five legendary Idaho characters who had nicknames.

8. Call the place you keep maps in your car a jockey box.

9. Own any gemstone found in the state.

10. Know the Idaho connection of at least five famous people.

STEP 1
IDAHO PLACE NAMES

Cataldo
Enaville Dworshak ONEIDA Palouse
MENAN Hammett TETON
Ahsahka IDAHO SHOSHONE
Kamiah Rathdrum Ucon Juliaetta
Notus Lapwai
Geneva FARRAGUT
BENEWAH Viola Weippe

A GUIDE TO IDAHO PLACE NAMES

You'll never be a real Idahoan until you learn how to pronounce the state's trickiest place names. I'm listing the most challenging and most interesting names, occasionally working a pronunciation guide into the sentence in place of the name itself to keep repetition at a minimum.

There are hundreds of other Idaho names you might want to learn. The book *Idaho Place Names, A Geographical Dictionary*, by Lalia Boone, is probably the best single source for such research. Unfortunately, it's no longer in print. I used Lalia's book a lot when compiling the following list. I also used the *Pronunciation Guide for the State of Idaho* by William J. Ryan. Sadly, it is so rare as to be practically non-existent. It was published by the Journalism Department of Idaho State University in 1975 to help keep broadcasters from making fools of themselves.

A

Acequia: The Idaho pronunciation is uh-SEEK-we-uh. Spanish language speakers would probably say a-SAKE-e-ya. It means canal or irrigation ditch in Spanish.

Ahsahka: Pronounced uh-SOCK-uh. It's Nez Perce for "fork in the river."

Athol: Be especially careful with this one. Named for an Indian chief, it is pronounced ATH-ul.

B

Basalt: If you're a geologist, you call that rock bu-SALT. If you live in this tiny Bingham County community, it's pronounced BAY-salt.

Benewah: Named after another Indian Chief, it is pronounced BEN-u-wah.

Boise: No Z. Really. One can debate why residents prefer the soft S in BOY-see, but you may as well stamp NOT FROM AROUND HERE on your forehead if you say BOY-zee.

Bruneau: BROO-no is the way to say it. Why are the town, the river, the canyon, and the state park called that? Maybe it's French for "dark water." Maybe it was named for a trapper by that name.

C

Cassia: Call it CASH-uh unless you're French. If you're from Paris (not the one in Idaho), you're welcome to say ka-shee-uh. It is peasant French for "raft," but there are other theories about where the name came from. Since the community of Raft River is in Cassia County, I'm going with that.

Cataldo: Named after missionary Father Joseph Cataldo, pronounce this one kuh-TAUL-doe.

Chatcolet: Often shortened to just "Chat" by the locals, say CHAT-koe-let. Some say it is Coeur d'Alene for "place where animals are trapped." It's in Benawah County, near Heyburn State Park.

Cocolalla: Try koe-koe-LAW-luh. It means very cold in Coeur d'Alene. The name is attached to several features in Bonner County.

Coeur d'Alene: Pronounce it kore-duh-LANE. Ironically, this isn't a Coeur d'Alene word. It was given to the Tribe by French trappers. "Heart of the Awl" is the literal meaning. It is said this somehow conveyed that Tribal members were shrewd traders.

THE IDAHO CONVERSION KIT

D

Desmet: Named after Father Pierre Jean De Smet, you should say dee-SMET. The missionary was so popular that another Idaho town tried to appropriate the name. Postal officials didn't want two Desmets in Idaho, arguing that could be confusing. So, the residents of that town decided to spell it backward, Temsed. For whatever reason, when the paperwork came back, officials had changed the spelling to Tensed. That stuck.

Detrich: Judge Frank S. Detrich said it was pronounced DEE-trick.

Dubois: The county seat of Idaho's least populated county, is pronounced DOO-boyss. That's the way Senator Dubois pronounced it. Away with your doo-BWAH, I say!

Dworshak: Named in honor of Senator Henry Dworshak, the dam is pronounced D-WORE-shack.

E

Egin: Allegedly, the Shoshone name for "cold" is pronounced EE-jin. It's a town in Fremont County.

Enaville: EE-nuh-vill is a good way to say it. The tiny town was named after Princess Ena, the daughter of Queen Victoria and later Queen of Spain. It was a supply station in Shoshone County in the 1880s.

F

Farragut: Admiral Farragut, who famously said, "Damn the torpedoes. Full speed ahead!" pronounced his name FAIR-uh-gut. This state park was a naval training station during WWII.

Fernan: It's a lake, it's creek, it's a ridge! And, it's pronounced fur-NAN.

G

Gannett: Unlike the newspaper company, this Blaine County community is GAN-net.

Geneva: Summits of high-ranking international officials are sometimes held in the Swiss town of the same name. In Idaho, you can go to Geneva Summit by driving up a hill. It is pronounced Juh-NEE-vuh.

H

Hamer: No, you can't drive nails with Hamer. Not enough Ms. HAY-mur.

Hammett: It has the Ms, so it's pronounced HAM-mut.

Heise: Famous for hot springs and pools, say HIGH-see.

Huetter: Near Post Falls, this town name sounds like HUT-ur.

I

Idavada: This might vary, depending on how you pronounce Nevada. It's a portmanteau, or the combining of two words, in this case, the state names of Idaho and Nevada. My source says eye-duh-VAY-da.

Indianola: You'll run across this name more often in Iowa than in Idaho. There, it's a town of about 15,000. Here, it's a Forest Service field station. You'll find the name in other states, too. Pronounce it Indian-NO-la.

THE IDAHO CONVERSION KIT

J

Jacques: Don't get all French about the name of this spot in the road. Say JACKS.

Juliaetta: When Postmaster Charles Snyder decided to combine the names of his two daughters, he came up with the prettiest town name in Idaho. Say joo-lee-ETT-uh.

K

Kalispell: The Montana town is better known, but Idaho has Kalispell Bay. It is pronounced KAL-iss-pell.

Kamiah: If you're looking for The Heart of the Monster, it's near Kamiah, pronounced KAM-ee-eye. That monster tale is the creation story of the Nez Perce.

Kaniksu: This means "black robe" in the language of the Coeur d'alenes. It refers to the missionaries who came West to tell their story. It is pronounced kun-NICK-sue.

Ketchum: David Ketchum built a cabin here in 1879. When the population justified a post office someone thought Leadville would be a good name. Too many Leadvilles, postal officials said. Ketchum, KETCH-um, was the second and better choice.

Keuterville: Henry Kuther wanted this little town named Kutherville. The bleary-eyed officials at the Post Office Department misread it. What they say goes. So, now we pronounce it KYOO-tur-vill.

Kimama: What is it with names in Idaho that start with a K? Wrap your tongue around kuh-MY-muh. Railroad officials who named the siding thought it meant "butterfly" in some Indian language.

Kooskia: This is easy to pronounce. Just leave off the last letter. KOOSS-kee. It means "where the waters join," in the Nez Perce language. Sort of. The original word is Kooskooskia.

Kootenai: KOO-tun-ay comes from the Kootenai Tribal word meaning "water people." The Kootenai Tribe started what was probably the last war with Indians in the U.S. They declared war on the government in 1974. Not a single shot was fired, but the action got them official recognition as a Tribe, something they knew they were since forever.

Kuna: This bustling community southwest of Boise is called KYOO-nuh. It was named by someone who thought it was an Indian word for "smoke." Or "snow." Or "the end." Or "Greenleaf." Or something.

L

Laclede: You'll find a lot of French place names in Idaho. Luh-KLEED was named after a French engineer.

Lago: LAY-go could be the Italian word for "lake" or an Indian word, the meaning of which has gone the way of so many Indian words.

Lanark: Near Bear Lake, LAN-ark is named for a town in Scotland.

Lapwai: Call it LAP-way. It's from a couple of Nez Perce words, lap-lap, meaning "butterfly," and wai meaning "stream."

Latah: LAY-taw, is the way to pronounce it. It's allegedly a Nez Perce word meaning "the place of pine trees and pestle." If a major part of your diet was camas roots, you might have a name like that for the place you ground those roots into flour.

THE IDAHO CONVERSION KIT

Leadore: Some Idaho place names are so simple that you wonder how you could mispronounce them. LED-ore is how you pronounce this one unless you pronounce it LEED-ore, which would be wrong.

Leonia: A railroad worker is said to have named it for his home in Italy. Lee-OWN-ee-uh.

Lochsa: This is said to be a Flathead Indian word meaning "rough water." Indeed, the river has some. Say LOCK-saw.

M

Mackay: This name famously gives newcomers fits. Pronounce it MACK-ee.

Malad: Two rivers and a town have this name. It is muh-LAD after the French "malady." A good demonstrative sentence of its meaning might be: "The trappers ate too much beaver tail, and it gave them a malady."

McCammon: Another name that came to Idaho via railroad. It, muh-KAM-un, was named after a railroad promoter.

Medimont: Remember that portmanteau in the listing for Idavada? Here's another. Medimont, MED-ih-mont is a combination of "medicine" and "mountain." Why they didn't just call it Medicine Mountain, as the nearby mountain is called, is a puzzle.

Menan: The Menan Buttes, muh-NAN, in Southeastern Idaho are two of the largest tuff cones in the world. Tuff is a rock made up of more than 75 percent volcanic ash.

Michaud: Michaud Flats, mish-ODD, is between American Falls and Pocatello. The irrigation project there goes by that name, as does a small phosphate-related Super Fund site.

Minidoka: We have lost the meaning of so many Indian names. This one, min-ih-DOKE-uh, is probably Indian, but there's a dispute over which language it came from before you even get to the dispute about what the word means. Maybe "well spring." Maybe "broad expanse."

Minnetonka: The definition of min-ee-TONKA-uh seems more certain than many. It seems to be from the Sioux language, with minne meaning "water" and tonka meaning "big." Minnetonka Cave is big—the biggest formation cave in Idaho. The water associated with this Bear Lake County wonder is just slow drips.

Mohler: Say MOE-lur. Named for a railroad guy, this was once a small town that is now more of an area in Lewis County.

Montour: The name, MAWN-toor, has hazy French roots. It once meant something like "a setting." It's in Gem County.

Montpelier: The better-known Montpelier, mawnt-PELL-yur, is in Vermont. That's where Brigham Young was from. He named the town in Bear Lake County.

Moscow: The easy way to remember how to pronounce Moscow is to remember that there are no cows there. Wait. That doesn't work. Still, it's pronounced MOSS-koe. It is one of about twenty towns that carry that name in the U.S. None of them claim a relationship to the one in Russia.

Moyie: You'll find the Moyie River, Moyie Springs, and Moyie Falls near Bonners Ferry. The name, MOY-ee, came from an area in British Columbia. It may mean "wet," or it could be a type of quartz.

THE IDAHO CONVERSION KIT

N

Nampa: Say NAM-puh. It probably means something like "footprint" or "big foot." The Shoshoni word seems not to have anything to do with a sasquatch.

Nezperce: Pronounce it nezz-PURSE, just like the two-word version. It means "pierced nose" in French. Trappers applied it to natives who already had a perfectly good name, Nimiipuu. The Tribe did not practice nose piercing, but the name stuck. Nezperce is the county seat of Lewis County.

Notus: I'll put you on notice that Notus is pronounced NO-tuss. What the name means is in dispute. Various stories have it as a Greek name, an Indian name, and a conjunction of Not Us. You pick.

O

Ola: Names sometimes just pop up. Take Ola, OH-luh, for example. It was allegedly named for an old Swede who just happened along when they were picking a new name for the post office.

Onaway: This Latah County community doesn't have much of a backstory for its name, ON-uh-way. It was named after a town in New York.

Oneida: Speaking of New York, Oneida County, oh-NYE-duh, was named for that state's Lake Oneida. That, in turn, was named for the Oneida Indians.

Oreana: With "ore" in the name, it's a good bet mining was involved in the naming oh-ree-ANNA. But don't take that bet. It's a Spanish word for an "unbranded but earmarked calf."

Orofino: On the other hand, or-uh-FEEN-oh, is all about the gold. It means "fine gold" in Spanish.

Orogrande: Pronounced or-uh-GRAND, this name has the same roots as Orofino. It was a popular one, being attached to a town in Custer County, another town in Idaho County, and a creek in Clearwater County.

Owyhee: Aloha. Pronounce this oh-WYE-hee and notice the similarity to the way you say Hawaii. No accident. The county was named for three island natives who went looking for beaver in the mountains and never came back. Americans were calling the people of what was then known as the Sandwich Islands, Owyhees.

P

Pahsimeroi: Pronouncing puh-SIMMER-eye is easier than spelling it. The river and the valley get their name from a Shoshoni word or words for "water," "grove," and "one." Think "one grove of trees on the water."

Paris: You already know how to pronounce this. What you may not know is that the name of the Idaho town has nothing to do with the home of the Eifel Tower. The town was named after Fredrick Perris, the man who platted it. Why they spelled it differently is open to question. Probably those scoundrel postal officials and their persnickety pens. They were always "helping" towns get their names right.

Palouse: Pronounce it puh-LOOSE, then argue about where the name came from. Pelouse, meaning "grassy" in French, seems like a good source. French trappers were terrorizing beavers and naming places for many years in what is now Idaho. A better explanation for the name is that it comes from the Sachaptin Indian name of a nearby village called, Palus. Either way, the Palouse is a rolling prairie now turned pioneer quilt with the squares of colored crops alternating, mostly in yellows and greens.

THE IDAHO CONVERSION KIT

Pegram: PEA-gram, located in Bear Lake County, was named for a railroad engineer.

Pend Orielle: Say pond-uh-RAY, and you'll be right. Named for an Indian Tribe that French trappers said wore earrings. That tribal description is now disputed by anthropologists. Some creative minds have pointed out that the lake—Idaho's deepest—looks something like an ear itself. However, naming it after its shape would have required at least a helicopter, if not an orbiting satellite.

Picabo: Named after Olympian Picabo Street ... Sorry, no, she was named after the Blaine County town of PEEK-uh-boo. It may be an Indian word whose definition has faded away.

Pingree: PING-gree was named after a developer. It's in Bingham County, about twenty minutes southwest of Blackfoot.

Plummer: Say it like you're calling someone to fix your leaky sink. It may be named after Henry Plummer, a notorious outlaw who had a hideout nearby. The Coeur d'Alene Tribal Headquarters is here.

Pocatello: This probably tops the list of Idaho odd names, though we're pretty used to it by now. The city, poe-kuh-TELL-oh, was named for a great Shoshoni leader. He never called himself that, but white settlers gave him the moniker for unknown reasons. One popular, though highly suspect, story is that he often came to town to pick up pork and tallow. It seems an obvious backformation meant to belittle a man who in no way deserved it.

Portneuf: The river by this name, PORT-nuff, flows through Pocatello. The river and various features in the area are named after a fur trapper.

Potlatch: It was a tradition among the Chinook tribes to exchange gifts at annual gatherings. POT-latch is the pronunciation of the word associated with those gatherings. It became attached to a town, a river, a creek, and a timber company.

R

Rathdrum: RATH-drum was not the first choice for the name of the town in Kootenai County that bears the name. Citizens wanted to call it Westwood. Postal officials—always trying to avoid confusion—decided there were already too many towns of that name. Residents opted for the Irish birthplace of one of their own as a second choice.

Reubens: I include ROO-buns only because we're a little short of towns in Idaho whose name begins with R. The name has an unexpected backstory. James Reubens, for whom the town is named, was a Nez Perce Indian who sided with US troops during the Nez Perce War of 1877.

S

Sagle: It's easy enough to say SAY-gull. What's interesting about the name of this town, near Sandpoint, is how it got its name. Those pesky post-office officials balked at naming the town Eagle because there was already another town named Eagle in Idaho. It wasn't the current town of Eagle, but it did have the first Eagle Post Office. Someone simply substituted an "S" for the first "E" in eagle.
That got the needed approval from the Post Office Department.

St. Maries: The name of the county seat of Benewah County, is called Saint MARYS. Father Pierre-Jean De Smet named the town in honor of the Virgin Mary.

Samaria: The town of suh-MARY-uh is more of an area these days. It lost its post office in 1983. Near Malad City, Samaria was named thus because residents were known as Good Samaritans.

Secesh: Many minors who worked in the area in Idaho County were from the Confederate states. Because they were secessionists, they were called "Secesh Doctrinaires." The name for the basin and the river is pronounced SEE-sesh.

THE IDAHO CONVERSION KIT

Shoshone: There's a town and a waterfall by this name in Southern Idaho and a county in Northern Idaho that goes by the same name. All are named for the Shoshoni Indians. Pronounce it show-SHOWN.

Skitwish: This peak in Kootenai County is pronounced just as it reads, SKIT-wish. I included it because it's fun to say and because the name is derived from the Coeur d'Alene word Skitswish. That's what they called their nation before French trappers started calling the Indians Coeur d'Alenes.

Tamarack: The western larch is also commonly called the TAM-uh-rack. There's a creek by that name in Clearwater County and there was an early settlement called that in Adams County. Today, it's most prominently attached to a ski resort on Lake Cascade.

Targhee: Early Idahoans loved Indian names, even though they tended to misinterpret them when they attached one to a town or feature. This is understandable since the indigenous people of the Northwest didn't have a written language. TAR-gee is a good example. In honoring a Bannock chief, the spelling of the name morphed from Ty-gee to Ti-ge, and finally to Targhee. The name is on a forest, a creek, and a ski resort. The latter is in Wyoming, but Idaho often lays claim to it since you can't get there from Wyoming.

Teton: If you're eleven, you probably snicker when you hear this word, knowing that it is French for "breast." The Tetons, firmly in Wyoming, are clearly visible from Idaho. They have lent their name, TEE-tawn, to a county, river, and town in Idaho. The latter is called Tetonia. Pronounce that tee-TOE-nee-uh.

Tyhee: This Bannock County town is on the Fort Hall Indian Reservation. TIE-hee is named for a Bannock leader. His name meant "swift."

U

Ucon: This is another Idaho town that owes its name to the postal people in Washington, DC. Citizens wanted to call it Elba, but bureaucrats pointed out there was already an Elba in the Big Book of Post Offices. Don't spend a lot of time looking for a copy. I just made that name up. As did postal officials when it came to choosing a name for YOU-con. Apparently, feeling generous, they gave residents of the little town a list of choices. Residents picked Ucon, which was something like an acronym for Union Pacific Mining Company.

V

Viola: They called her VI-oh-luh. She was the first child born in the community, then became the first schoolteacher there. When her father became the first postmaster, naming the Latah County community Viola just seemed right.

W

Waha: This is an Indian word that means, maybe, "beautiful" or "subterranean water." WAAH-haw is in Nez Perce County. It was a town and a valley and a lake.

Wapello: What were they thinking when they named this little community in Bingham County? Chief wah-PELL-oh was a Fox Indian. The Tribe lived in the Midwest.

Wasatch: The WAH-satch Mountain Range is mostly in Utah but stretches into the Bear Lake country. It is a Ute word for "mountain pass."

Weippe: This word, one of Idaho's most-often mispronounced, is an Indian term for "gathering place." Pronounce it WEE-ipe.

Weiser: We'll end with another oft-bungle name. WEE-zur is the county seat of Washington County.

THE TROUBLESOME PHANTOM Z

There is, perhaps, no quicker way to set a long-time resident of Boise's teeth to grinding than to call the town "Boy-zee." If you don't pronounce it "Boy-see," slap yourself in the face with your iPad right now.

Even so, audiences usually overlook the faux pas when the star on stage panders out to the crowd, "Hello, Boy-zee!" Unless, of course, they happen to be on stage in Pocatello at the time.

In the summer of 2010, Jewel played at Outlaw Field in Boise and endeared herself to the audience, in spite of a couple of false starts, by singing a newly penned title, *The Boise Song*. The lyrics list letters you can find in the names of certain cities, i.e., an A in Atlanta, a Y in Kansas City, etc., but ending each verse with "But there is no Z in Boise."

You can easily find it with Google, but if you missed that concert, you might never hear her perform it live unless she comes back to Idaho. According to setlist.com, which covers concert statistics, Jewel has performed it just that one time in public.

If you do a search for Boise in the lyrics of songs, you'll come up with about fifty occurrences. Many are versions of the same song brought out on different albums. Most are obscure.

What's Your Name by Lynyrd Skynyrd made a big splash with the opening line, "It's eight o'clock in Boy-zee, Idaho," released in 1977. According to songfacts.com, the original line to that song was "It's eight o'clock and boys it's time to go." Ronnie Van Zant's brother, Don Van Zant, opened the national tour of his band, .38 Special, in Boise. Ronnie, who wrote the song, changed the line to fit the venue.

Three days after the album containing the song was released, three members of Lynyrd Skynyrd, including Ronnie Van Zant, were killed in a plane crash. *What's Your Name*, peaked on the Billboard chart at number thirteen in March 1978, probably making it the most popular song containing a reference to the state. It appeared on nine Lynyrd Skynyrd albums.

Boise popped up in the lyrics to a Harry Chapin song, *WOLD*. Those were the call letters of the Boise radio station where the singer/DJ had hit rock bottom. As a former Boise DJ, I probably resent the implication. Chapin ignored the fact that all radio station call letters west of the Mississippi begin with a K. In the east, you'll find W call letters, with the exception of KDKA in Pittsburgh. But I digress. Oh, the song made it to number thirty-four on the Hot One Hundred.

Drake (featuring Lil Wayne and Andre 3000) obliquely mentioned Boise in the 2011 song, *The Real Her*. It was a little hat-tip to the Blue Turf. The word was a little on the fence Z/S-wise but would probably make a native smile.

STEP 2
THE SHAPE OF IDAHO

the 42nd parallel

IDAHO'S FIRST BORDER

What would one day become Idaho was the last of 50 states to be entered by Euro-Americans. On August 12, 1805, Meriwether Lewis and his advance party of the Corps of Discovery crossed into future Idaho. Importantly, they also crossed out of the Louisiana Purchase they were sent to explore and into territory claimed by Spain.

Spain's claims were a bit tenuous. Fourteen years later, they would evaporate in negotiations with Secretary of State John Quincy Adams. Spain would be embroiled in civil war by this time, leaving it without troops to vigorously defend its claims. President James Monroe was more interested in acquiring Florida from Spain than the distant and, perhaps, worthless lands of the Pacific Northwest. Spain's claim to Florida was practically ancient compared with its hold on the Western lands of North America. The country's hold on Florida dated back to 1513 when Juan Ponce de Leon sailed to the peninsula, naming it La Florida, the "land of flowers."

Secretary Adams was adamant about the young country stretching from coast to coast and negotiated much longer than the president would have preferred. Finally, on February 22, 1819, Spanish Minister Plenipotentiary to the United States Luis do Onis met with Secretary of State Adams to sign a treaty. They had agreed that Spain would give up Florida but also that the two countries would settle on the 42nd Parallel west of the Pacific Ocean as the boundary between their territories.

Florida and Idaho have little else in common, but they came under the United States' dominion on the same day. That 1819 treaty set the southern border of what would become Idaho and Oregon. My source for this piece is the very readable book, *Inventing Idaho*, by Keith C. Peterson. Add it to your library as you feel yourself becoming more and more of an Idahoan. Put it right next to *Idaho for the Curious*, by Cort Conley.

The shape of Idaho just wants to be noticed. And it has a legend!

IDAHO'S UNIQUE SHAPE

So, every state has a unique shape. Even Wyoming and Colorado are different-sized rectangles. *By the way, what's with those two?* It's like map makers just got bored at the end of the day and drew four lines with their T-squares. Even Kansas, as one-dimensional as a sheet of paper, has a little oops in the upper right-hand corner where Missouri slouches into it.

But I digress.

The shape of Idaho just wants to be noticed. It has that gnome-sitting-in-a-chair thing going for it. Its face stares into Montana while Montana rudely stares into Idaho's belly. It's one of a handful of states that extends more vertically than horizontally as if it is always in ascension.

And it has a legend.

In 1863, when Idaho became a territory, its boundaries included most of Wyoming and all of Montana. That didn't last long, though. Congress carved Montana out of Idaho Territory in May 1864, choosing the Bitterroot Mountain Range as the main border between the two territories.

Somehow, though, a legend grew up that the boundary was the result of a surveying error. According to this tale, the border was supposed to follow the Continental Divide all the way to Canada. Idaho would have included Missoula, Butte, and all of Montana west of the Rockies—a nice little piece of land.

The story goes that the surveyors were drunk or had been paid off by agents from Montana who wanted a bigger territory. It's a good story, but it isn't true. In fact, the boundary between Montana and Idaho wasn't even officially surveyed until fourteen years after Idaho's statehood. The states simply got along, knowing that the border generally followed the crest of the Bitterroots, as designated by the U.S. Congress.

In the years leading up to statehood, there was a lot of haggling and political maneuvering over where Idaho's borders should be. But drunken surveying crews did not play a part in shaping the state.

One footnote. I'm told the boundary legend tale came about because surveyors habitually dropped their empty refreshment bottles in the hole when they placed survey markers.

MORE ABOUT SHAPES

The first thing you should do to become a genuine Idahoan is learn the shape of the state. Below are eight stylized shapes. Here, you'll find the correct answer and some verbiage meant to soothe or shame you if you got it wrong.

Check your calendar. If it's 1863, then this one is correct. When President Abraham Lincoln signed the bill creating Idaho Territory on March 4, 1863, this is what it looked like. It included all of what would later become Montana and Wyoming. The territory was bigger than Texas and, for a few months, was the largest US Territory.

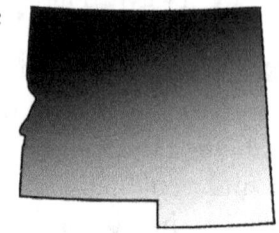

THE IDAHO CONVERSION KIT

In 1864, Idaho Territory went on a serious diet. Congress wisely decided that one Texas was plenty, thank you very much. Northeast Idaho Territory became Montana Territory that year. At the same time, Idaho lost most of Wyoming.

Idaho Territory slimmed up again in 1868, losing the love handle on the east that would become part of Wyoming. This is what Idaho looks like today. Pat yourself on the back if you chose this one.

This *could* be what Idaho looks like tomorrow if tomorrow is defined as "probably never." When this book was written, there was something called the Greater Idaho Movement. Proponents, most of whom live in rural Oregon, so love Idaho's scenic beauty that they just have to be a part of it. In writing circles, the preceding sentence is called a "lie." Those secessionist Oregonians admire Idaho's conservative politics and would love to thumb their collective noses at Salem, Oregon's capital city, and the progressive politics in general on that side of the Cascades. Similar schemes to rejigger Idaho's borders have popped up in the past. They have consistently failed because every state government involved in the proposal has to approve it, then Congress has to approve it.

If you chose this as the shape of
Idaho, you are geographically
challenged, but you are not alone.
This is Iowa. One would think Iowa
would change its name since three of
the letters it contains are currently in
use by Idaho. Some wags might point
out that Iowa had those letters first,
which is technically correct. Idaho, indisputably, wears them
better. Iowa, you should consider Cornucopia, a lovely name
implying abundance.

Please say you didn't choose this one.
That's Ohio. It, too, shares three letters
with the State of Idaho. Frankly, we're
getting a little tired of that. See above.
Pick your own dang name.

You could almost be forgiven
for picking this shape. Montana
is practically begging to stick
its nose in this upside-down
image of Florida.

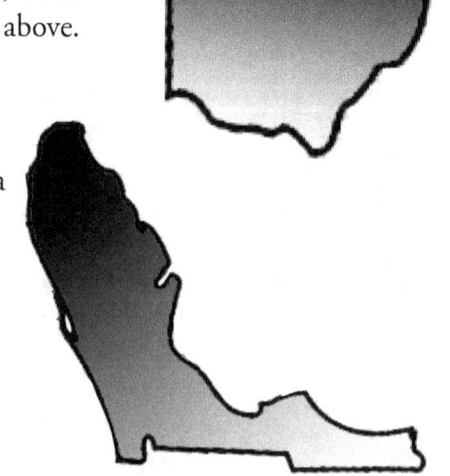

THE IDAHO CONVERSION KIT

If you chose this map, you may be from Mayberry. An upside-down map of Idaho hung on the wall of the sheriff's office in some of the old Andy Griffith shows on TV. It may have been meant to be the outline of the fictional town of Mayberry or the fictional county it was in. A map of Nevada got the same treatment in at least one episode. The map used most often for the background in those office scenes was one of Cincinnati.

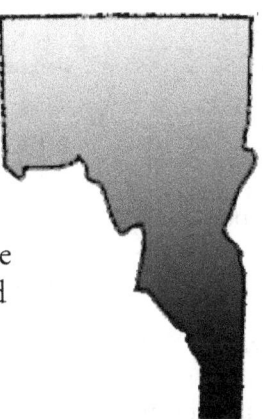

BORDER GRAVES

It's well-known that Idaho's first permanent settlement, the town of Franklin, was settled by pioneers, who thought they were still in Utah. They discovered their mistake only after a survey placed the border a bit south of them. *Welcome to Idaho!*

One of those "Welcome to Idaho" signs is on I-15 on the border south of Malad City. Just up the hill from that sign, on the Idaho side of the border, are two graves, each with a grave-sized fence around it. Neither of the occupants of the graves was from Franklin, but one could be forgiven for wondering. The dying wish for both was to be buried in Utah. Oops.

Hugh Moon was the first to find himself permanently located on the wrong side of the border. Mr. Moon was born in England in

1815. In 1840, he joined the Church of Jesus Christ of Latter-Day Saints and sailed to the United States. He was a devout Mormon, who at one time served as a bodyguard for Joseph Smith. Keep that tidbit of trivia in mind.

Moon was married in 1848 in Utah. Brigham Young had him move to Dixie in southern Utah to strengthen the church community there. Later, he and his family moved to Henderson Creek in Idaho Territory. It was there that he died. He considered Utah to be Zion, and he wanted to be buried there. His family, doing their best to honor his wishes, chose a gravesite on a hillside overlooking Cherry Creek south of Malad. The border survey would come later.

Hugh Moon wasn't the only one who wanted to be buried in Utah. Jane Copeland Howell, born in Illinois in 1789, became a resident of Idaho Territory in 1868. She had moved there with her son and his family. They had lived in Kaysville, Utah, for five years previously. Jane Howell had some affinity for Utah, though she wasn't LDS. She begged her family to see that she was buried there, not in Idaho, where she had lived for only a short time. They did their best, locating her gravesite near that of Hugh Moon, probably assuming Moon's relatives knew what they were doing. Again, the border survey proved them wrong.

There is something of an urban legend attached to the graves. As is often the case with such things, the story has a nubbin of truth. The legend has it that the two graves belonged to bodyguards of Brigham Young, who inexplicably hated Utah so much that they asked to be buried in Idaho. The truth nubbin was that Hugh Moon was the bodyguard of a church leader, Joseph Smith.

If there's a moral to this story, it's probably one that would rarely be useful today: Make sure the survey is complete before you commit to eternity in Utah.

STEP 3
IDAHO LICENSE PLATES

Scenic IDAHO
1A WJ785
FAMOUS POTATOES

COUNTY LICENSE PLATE DESIGNATORS

Any Idaho native can tell you where a car is from "just by looking at its license plate!" And, it's not even magic. Most personal vehicles have a "county designator" on their license plates. They're alphabetical starting with 1A, for Ada County, and going all the way through W for Washington County. Personalized plates don't display a county designator. Here's a handy guide to the counties, courtesy of the Idaho Department of Transportation. Keep it in your jockey box, which you totally have now that you live in Idaho (see page 143). *County seats are in parentheses.*

1A	Ada (Boise)	4C	Cassia (Burley)
2A	Adams (Council)	5C	Clark (Dubois)
1B	Bannock (Pocatello)	6C	Clearwater (Orofino)
2B	Bear Lake (Paris)	7C	Custer (Challis)
3B	Benewah (St. Maries)	E	Elmore (Mtn Home)
4B	Bingham (Blackfoot)	1F	Franklin (Preston)
5B	Blaine (Hailey)	2F	Fremont (St. Anthony)
6B	Boise (Idaho City)	1G	Gem (Emmett)
7B	Bonner (Sandpoint)	2G	Gooding (Gooding)
8B	Bonneville (Idaho Falls)	1	Idaho (Grangeville)
9B	Boundary (Bonners Ferry)	1J	Jefferson (Rigby)
10B	Butte (Arco)	2J	Jerome (Jerome)
1C	Camas (Fairfield)	K	Kootenai (Coeur d'Alene)
2C	Canyon (Caldwell)	1L	Latah (Moscow)
3C	Caribou (Soda Springs)	2L	Lemhi (Salmon)

3L	Lewis (Nez Perce)	**1P**	Payette (Payette)
4L	Lincoln (Shoshone)	**2P**	Power (American Falls)
1M	Madison (Rexburg)	**S**	Shoshone (Wallace)
2M	Minidoka (Rupert)	**1T**	Teton (Driggs)
N	Nez Perce (Lewiston)	**2T**	Twin Falls (Twin Falls)
1O	Oneida (Malad City)	**V**	Valley (Cascade)
2O	Owyhee (Murphy)	**W**	Washington (Weiser)

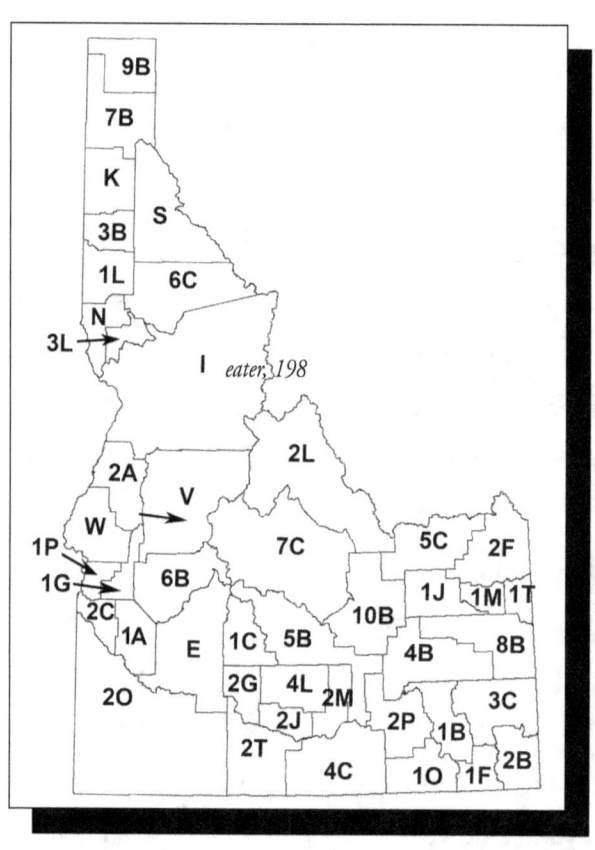

County designator map courtesy Idaho Department of Transportation

STEP 4
IDAHO SYMBOLS

*Spuds: Idaho's famous, world-famous, marketable, edible potatoes.
Photo: The Spud Drive-In between Victor and Driggs, Idaho.*

ON NAMES, NICKNAMES, MOTTOS, POTATOES, AND PLATES

What's in a name? No, I will not totally go Shakespeare on you. This is about Idaho, in particular the name of the state. When I was in fourth grade, I learned that the word "Idaho" meant "gem of the mountains." It was an Indian word, my teacher said. But Mrs. Adameck was wrong.

Many of us were taught that the name Idaho came from the Indian word "E-Da-How." That Indian word meant "Gem of the Mountains," or "light coming down the mountains," or something similar.

However, researchers say there wasn't a word like that in any Native American language. It turns out the name Idaho was simply invented by someone who thought it sounded Indian.

George M. Willing came up with the word Idaho in 1860. He lobbied to have it become the name for what is now Colorado. He told people it was an Indian word that meant "gem of the mountains." That state might have been called Idaho, but someone discovered the name had been invented. The new territory became Colorado, which means colored or red in Spanish. The near name still lingers as the moniker of Idaho Springs.

When it came time to name our new territory in 1863, Congress was about to call it Montana, but the name Idaho cropped up again. By that time, the Nation's leaders had forgotten that Idaho was a made-up name. An Oregon senator convinced his colleagues to abandon the name Montana because the word meant nothing at all. Idaho, he said, meant "gem of the mountains."

And the new territory was named Idaho.

Meanwhile, as you may know, the name Montana, which means something like mountainous in Spanish and Latin, was used for another territory.

Through all this, it seemed to not occur to anyone why there was a need for a single word that meant "gem of the mountains" in the first place.

So, my fourth-grade teacher wasn't wrong when she told me what Idaho meant. It was the conventional wisdom of the time until renowned Idaho historian Merle Wells discovered the history of the name a few years later. A name that means quite a lot to Idahoans today.

So, now that we knew what to call it, people decided the state also needed a nickname. Often a nickname is shorter than a given name, i.e., Bob is short for Robert, and Jim for James. Given just that parameter, Idaho would probably be called Ida. That didn't ever catch on.

Idaho's nickname grew out of the supposed meaning of the word that George Willing invented. His definition, "gem of the mountains," got shortened to The Gem State. That one stuck. All states have nicknames, but only seven, including Idaho, seem sure enough of themselves to need only one nickname.

Although the name Idaho was considered for three states and had no actual meaning, its purported meaning fit the state well. People have found jasper, opal, jade, topaz, zircon, tourmaline, star garnets, and even diamonds in The Gem State. Some have made the bold claim that every known gemstone can be found in Idaho. There are some 300 gemstones. I'm still waiting to see that 300-stone Idaho collection.

So, now with a name and a nickname, we're ready for business, right? Not quite. Every state has a motto, most of them in Latin. Idaho fell in with the majority, choosing *Esto Perpetua*, or "Let it be perpetual" or "Be eternal" as the state motto.

An odd sidebar to this is that Secretary of State George Curtis thought the definition was not quite right, so in 1942 he ran a contest asking citizens to come up with a more "suitable" definition. A twelve-year-old girl from Lava Hot Springs, Etheleen E. Evans, wrote a patriotic letter suggesting the definition be "May she be forever under Old Glory." That won the heart of the secretary of state, but it fell flat with the public.

Definitions do change, but one advantage of using the dead Latin language is that it stays much the same as it has been for centuries. This is useful when you want someone who speaks Portuguese and understands Latin to get the meaning of your concept. It doesn't work so well if you want to discuss Tupperware. So, hurray for the first part of that Lava Hot Springs girl's definition. Boo for the second part, patriotic as it may be. There's just nothing about a flag in *Esto Perpetua*.

This brings us to the state flag of Idaho. Since it is largely the state seal centered on a blue background, one would think we would have had an Idaho state flag for as long as we've had a seal since 1891. Not so.

It took the Legislature seventeen years to pass a law creating an Idaho State Flag. Even then they punted to the adjutant general, delegating the duty of coming up with the design and specifying that the flag would be blue and have the word Idaho on it. They appropriated 100 dollars to make that happen on March 12, 1907.

It seemed odd to me that they put 100 dollars in the adjutant general's budget. *Why would he need anything?* He could just send a flag company a picture of the state seal and tell them how it was supposed to appear on flags. Voila! Make some flags!

My misunderstanding was that the 100 dollars was for the cost of making a single flag. The state wasn't planning on waving a flag

Anyone can buy an Idaho State flag nowadays. This one was the first one manufactured and held special importance for many years. It is preserved by the Idaho State Historical Society. This photo is in the society's physical photo collection in Boise.

THE IDAHO CONVERSION KIT

from every courthouse in Idaho. The Legislature had the adjutant general design and then order one flag.

Idaho got along with a single official state flag for years. It made the headlines in 1926 that the flag was traveling out of state with Governor C.C. Moore so that both could attend the governors' conference in Cheyenne. The stay-at-home flag had only traveled out of state a couple of times before that. It lived in the governor's office when not visiting other states. Today that original flag is in the possession of the Idaho State Historical Society.

Are we done yet with how we let the world know about this place called Idaho? Not quite. Go read your license plate.

Idaho doesn't have an official slogan, as some states do, but it might as well be "Famous Potatoes," the slogan that graces most Idaho license plates.

A tip of the hat to the Idaho Potato Commission for their tireless efforts to keep that slogan on the plates. Also, a blatting raspberry to the Idaho Potato Commission for their efforts, etc., etc. One can love potatoes and still prefer not to be a rolling advertisement for them. I fall into that camp. Many of us like-minded folks have discovered that certain specialized and personalized plates do not carry the slogan. In the late 1980s, that wasn't the case. I took on the slogan in a way that I hoped would be viewed as humorous by my many friends and family members in Bingham County who raise potatoes.

Potatoes started showing up on Idaho plates in 1948. The slogan on the bottom of the plates that year and the following year was "World Famous Potatoes." In case that was too subtle for you,

Idaho license plate with a yummy-looking baked potato, 1948.

A bigger, fluffier, even more yummy potato with a tad more butter, 1949.

the silver plates featured a large, full-color baked potato sticker slapped in the middle of the plate.

The hot potato was dropped in 1950, along with the slogan. The slogan came back in 1953, disappeared in '54 and '55, and came back in '56. In 1957 "World" was dropped from the slogan, making it "Famous Potatoes." That's the slogan that has stuck ever since.

Did I tell you how much I love potatoes? Love 'em. Not so much on my license plates, though. So, in the late 1980s my brother, Kent Just, and I set out to give Idahoans a choice. I located the company that made the reflective material used on the license plates at that time and learned that you could buy it in strips. I ordered a roll of the stuff and had slogans printed on it in the same size, font, and color as the slogan on the license plates. Buyers could peel off the paper on the back and stick the new slogan over "Famous Potatoes." We sold them for a couple of bucks through Stinker Stations. You could pick from "Famous Potholes," "The Whitewater State," and several others.

Kent acted as the front man on this project because I was working for the State of Idaho at the time and was a little unsure about how my employer would take this little prank. We got publicity for the project in papers from Washington State to Washington DC.

THE IDAHO CONVERSION KIT

Some articles made it sound like we had a factory cranking these out by the thousands. No. I had a roll of stickers and a pair of scissors.

Kent dropped in on Idaho's attorney general, whom we both knew. We thought we might get a little free advice about the legality of the stickers. The AG, we'll give him the pseudonym of "Jim" to protect the innocent, said to Kent, "You were never here."

Encouraging people to put an unauthorized sticker on a license plate ruffled the feathers of the folks over at Idaho State Police HQ. They made noises about it sufficient to make us stop selling them. We were certain we were on solid legal ground because the US Supreme Court had already ruled that it was legal to cover up a license plate slogan in the name of free speech (New Hampshire's "Live Free or Die"). Still, it didn't seem worthwhile to hire a lawyer for a $150 joke. We'd had our fun, and we'd already made our money back. Nowadays I'm content to display a potato-free personalized plate, no longer a scofflaw.

By the way, you will not be shocked to learn that Idaho has a state vegetable and that it is the potato. You may wonder why it took until 2002 for the Legislature to make it so.

CAN YOU SPOT THIS IDAHO SYMBOL?

Idaho is horse country and has been for over 250 years. Idaho even stakes a claim to a breed, the Appaloosa.

The Appaloosa horse can be traced back to the Mongols in ancient China. It is the oldest identifiable horse breed. It wasn't called the Appaloosa until it became associated with the place later known as Idaho. The horses were well known on the Palouse prairie of northern Idaho, and over the years, those Palouse horses became known as *Appaloosas*.

ApHC Dreamfinder: Idaho's state horse is the Appaloosa. Not specifically this Appaloosa, though we could do worse. This is a photo of Dreamfinder, an iconic stallion of the breed inducted into the Appaloosa Horse Club Hall of Fame in 1996, courtesy of ApHC.

THE IDAHO CONVERSION KIT

The spotted horses came to the Northwest through Mexico. Spanish conquistadors lost or traded away enough of them to assure thriving herds in the new world. The Shoshone Tribe had them first, but it was the Nez Perce who perfected the breed.

Horses gave the Nez Perce an expanded range and produced a whole new way of living for them. They became buffalo hunters and developed trade relationships with other tribes far removed from their traditional range.

The Appaloosa was nearly lost when the great Nez Perce herds were split up and scattered following the Nez Perce War. An ambitious plan to save the horses brought the breed back from near extinction in the 1930s.

Today, thousands of the tough little horses with spotted blankets on their rear quarters can be seen in Idaho and around the world. If you visit Moscow, Idaho, don't miss the Appaloosa Museum, where you can learn the complete story of the breed that became Idaho's State Horse in 1975.

IDAHO HAS A CUTTHROAT SYMBOL

You can enjoy Idaho's state fish on your license plate, or on your dinner plate. Displaying the latter helps fund the Nongame Wildlife section of Idaho Fish and Game. Management of game animals is funded through the purchase of hunting and fishing licenses.

Photo of cutthroat trout (Onchorhynchus clarkii) *from the Idaho Department of Fish and Game's website, by Robert Sivinski, CalPhotos.*

Idaho is famous for trout. We raise more trout for restaurants than any other state. Clear Springs Foods in Buhl raises over 20 million pounds of them every year. But it's our equally famous catchable trout that fishermen love.

Idaho Fish and Game stocks over 30 million fish each year in the state's lakes and streams. Most of them are rainbow trout or kokanee salmon.

Our four main native trout include the rainbow, the bull trout, the cutthroat, and the steelhead.

People are most familiar with rainbow trout. Idaho's record rainbow trout was a 20-pound monster caught in the Snake River in 2009.

Unlike the rest of their native trout cousins, steelhead spend part of their life in the ocean, as much as 1800 miles from where they were hatched. Idaho's record steelhead was caught in the Clearwater River in 1973. It weighed just over 30 pounds.

The bull trout, or Dolly Varden, is an even bigger fish. The Idaho record is 32 pounds. That one was caught in Lake Pend Oreille in 1949. It's a record that will stand for a while. It is no longer legal to harvest a bull trout. You can catch them, you just can't keep them.

According to biologists, the first native Idaho trout was a cutthroat that swam into our waters about a million years ago. Cutthroat are very aggressive eaters, so they're easy to catch. The biggest one caught in our state weighed just shy of 19 pounds. It was pulled out of Bear Lake in 1970. The cutthroat—in general, not that specific fish—became Idaho's state fish in 1990.

Idaho's state fish, the cutthroat trout, is one of several wildlife license plates sponsored by the Idaho Fish and Wildlife Foundation. The fish joins an elk and a bluebird as wildlife icons on the license plates. In 1992, the Idaho Legislature passed a bill that allowed a portion of the sales proceeds to benefit the Idaho Fish and Game Department's nongame wildlife program, conservation education, and Watchable Wildlife.

Have you noticed all those non-natives moving into the state? So has the state bird. When I say non-native, I'm referring to invasive species such as sparrows and starlings. They tend to take all the good nesting sites away from our mountain bluebirds. You can help by buying a bluebird license plate or building and installing bluebird boxes if your place is big enough to suit the needs of the bluebirds.

Photo of the Mountain Bluebird (Sialia currucoides) *from the Idaho Department of Fish and Game's public information webpages by Blake Matheson, 2006 (NC, Flickr: EOL images).*

THE BLUEBIRD PROBABLY NOT ON YOUR SHOULDER

In 1931, the Legislature named the mountain bluebird as Idaho's state bird. There are two kinds of bluebirds in Idaho, the western bluebird, and the larger mountain bluebird.

The male mountain bluebird has a bright blue back, a paler blue body, and a whitish belly. The female is a gray-brown bird with a trace of blue on her wings, rump, and tail.

Bluebirds live throughout Idaho in high desert juniper, meadows in forested areas, in mountain valleys, and along open ridges. Most live above 4,000 feet. Their favorite food is the grasshopper.

There are plenty of grasshoppers in Idaho for them to eat, but bluebirds have a problem. And you can help.

Bluebirds like to nest in holes that woodpeckers and other animals have excavated. Vacant holes are getting scarce. Many trees with suitable nesting holes have been cut for firewood, burned, or removed for development. The good tree holes that remain are often taken by starlings and sparrows, two non-native species that tend to bully the gentle bluebirds away.

That's the bad news. The good news is that bluebirds love to move into a nice, new, wooden nesting box that you can provide them. The boxes are easy to build, and the Idaho Fish and Game Department has a free brochure that will tell you how to do it. They're fussy about where they nest, so if you live in town, don't bother with a box. They like rural areas away from buildings.

OUR DECISIVE SALAMANDER

Idaho has its share of state symbols, ranging from the Appaloosa horse to the Idaho giant salamander. One can argue about whether we need as many symbols as we have or any at all. I will stay away from that one.

It offers a good excuse to talk about an amazing creature that is found almost nowhere else. The Idaho giant salamander lives only in Idaho and in a small area of western Montana. It's a giant only in comparison with other salamanders, coming in at about 13 inches. It can be found in streams and rivers doing mostly what it does best, eating. It has a voracious appetite, but as long as you have a spine you're not likely prey. They eat mostly invertebrates.

Idaho giant salamanders are incredible animals and are best known for one peculiar trick. Most of them live their lives in streams scarfing down snails and such, but a small percentage of them find life on land a better gig. It's not that they go back and forth. They're either stream dwellers that have the necessary gills for that, or they live out their life on land, losing their gills and developing lungs. The land-dwelling salamanders develop a different, more upright body stance. Their head changes shape and their eyes take up a new position. Even their color changes. Most people looking at a stream-dweller and a land-dweller together would swear they were completely different species.

The Idaho giant salamander became Idaho's official amphibian in 2015, following five years of lobbying efforts by persistent Idaho teen Ilah Hickman. To learn more about the Idaho giant salamander, Google "Windows on Wildlife: Giant Salamander."

Salamander photos by Dr. John Cossel Jr.

AN EQUUS IS AN EQUUS, OF COURSE, OF COURSE

The Hagerman Horse, so named by locals, was discovered in 1928. Scientists call it *Equus simplicidens*. Five nearly-complete skeletons and 100 skulls were retrieved from a hillside across the Snake River near the town of Hagerman. Some paleontologists speculate that a herd of the horses may have been caught in flooding waters and drowned at the site. The Hagerman site remains the largest single discovery of this fossil found, and it is the earliest example of Equus, the genus that includes all modern horses, donkeys, and zebras. Even Mr. Ed.

It's not all about the horses at the Hagerman site. Preserved within the sediments is one of the most diverse deposits of Pliocene animals. Over 100 species of vertebrates, including 18 fish, four amphibians, nine reptiles, 27 birds, and 50 mammals have been identified, as well as freshwater snails, clams, and plant pollen. Idaho Department of Parks and Recreation owned and operated the site for a few years. It was traded for land that became Castle Rocks State Park in 2003. The National Park Service operates the site today as the Hagerman Fossil Beds National Monument.

Not every state has a state fossil, but Idaho does. It is a horse, of course, of course, the Hagerman Horse, named the state fossil in 1988.

This photo from 1968, shows Bob Romig, curator of collections at the Idaho State Historical Society examining the skeleton of what is probably Idaho's most famous fossil. The Hagerman Horse was a zebra-like creature about the size of a present-day Arabian horse. Idaho Statesman *photo.*

According to the Idaho Panhandle National Forest visitor brochure, "Idaho and India are the only two places in the world where star garnets are found in abundance. The 12-sided (dodecahedron) or 24-sided (trapezohedron) crystals range in size from sand-sized particles to golf balls or larger, and often have 4- or 6-ray stars when cut "en cabochon" by a lapidarist."

The public can collect these at the unique Forest Service's Emerald Creek Garnet Area in a safe and environmentally friendly way. Due to concerns for water quality, aquatic habitat, and public safety, the Forest Service now uses sluice boxes for enthusiasts to search for garnets. Get your tickets to the Garnet Area by reservation only through recreation.gov.

Photo of raw Idaho star garnets courtesy Visit Idaho, Steven Andrews.
Cut star garnet photo by Christine Plourde, published on many websites and news stories.

IDAHO'S UNIQUE ROCK STAR

The Gem State's best-known gemstone is the star garnet. Garnets are usually a dark purple or plum color. Some call the stone "red gold."

Garnets are not especially rare. They're commonly found in metamorphic rocks. However, star garnets are rare. They have been discovered in only two places on Earth, India and Idaho. That's why the 1967 Idaho legislature made the star garnet the official state gemstone.

Most star garnets have four rays that seem to shimmer and float across the surface of the polished stone as it's moved in the light. But the rarest of the rare have six rays or arms in the star. Collectors covet the beautiful six-ray garnet—found only in northern Idaho.

You can dig for star garnets yourself if you're the adventurous type. You're likely to be digging somewhere near Emerald Creek, so named because . . . garnets. Apparently, someone thought the reddish gems were emeralds. The digging is regulated by the U.S. Forest Service, and it requires an inexpensive permit. You can even hire an outfitter who will guarantee you find at least one cuttable garnet. The Moscow Chamber of Commerce can give you information. Maybe you'll be lucky enough to find a rare six-ray star garnet. There's not much point looking anywhere else but Idaho.

OUR MIGRATING MONARCHS

Did *you know Idaho has a state insect?* Yes, as do 44 other states. Many of them have two state insects, so stand by for legislation.

Idaho's state insect is the monarch butterfly made official in 1992. Monarchs get around, so it may not surprise you that it is also the state insect of Vermont, Texas, Minnesota, Illinois, West Virginia, and Alabama.

Monarchs, or *Danaus plexippus*, if you want to get all Latin, rely on milkweed in their larval stage. As adult butterflies, they feed on a variety of nectar-producing plants, accidentally spreading around pollen at the same time.

You probably know that monarchs migrate south for the winter. Western monarchs, those found in Idaho, typically over-winter in southern California, mostly around Pacific Grove. It's not the same butterfly coming back in the spring that you waved farewell to in October. It takes three or four generations of butterflies to make a migration loop.

Many Idahoans can identify a monarch caterpillar. Or, can you? It surprised me to learn that there are a series of five stages of growth for a monarch in the larval form. The first caterpillar to hatch from those tiny butterfly eggs is translucent green and less than a quarter of an inch long. It eats ferociously, then molts, revealing the beginnings of the white, black, and yellow markings we are familiar with. It eats again, and molts again, etc. until it reaches the fifth and Final stage and its ultimate size, about two inches long.

An adult monarch is a distinctive orange with black branching stripes leading to black wing edges with a double outline of white dots. If you see one that looks significantly smaller than you'd expect (a wingspan of about three-and-a-half to four inches), it's not a baby butterfly (no such thing). It's probably a viceroy butterfly.

Milkweed, which is unfortunately often considered a weed, is essential in the life cycle of the monarch. So, if you can let the plants grow, you'll be helping Idaho's official insect.

The Monarch butterfly, Idaho's state insect, spends summers in Idaho and then migrates to southern California for the winter. Photo by Allen Dale.

Val Kilmer may not have known it was a reference to Idaho's state fruit when he uttered the words, "I'm your huckleberry" while playing Doc Holliday in the 1993 movie Tombstone. The antiquated phrase has enjoyed something of a resurgence since then. You can buy any number of t-shirts with that line artistically printed on them. Some like huckleberries (or maybe just that quote) so much that they've had it tattooed on their bodies.

"I'M YOUR HUCKLEBERRY"

According to Victoria Wilcox, who has done way more research on the topic than I have the patience for, the phrase "I'm your huckleberry" has a proud literary tradition. Walter Noble Burns used the nineteenth-century slang phrase in his 1927 novel, *Tombstone: The Iliad of the Southwest*. It was an early novel about the Earp brothers and Doc Holliday. The phrase means something like, "I'm the man for the job" or "I'm your hero." Val Kilmer uttered the same phrase in the 1993 movie *Tombstone*, which was based on the aforementioned book and written by Kevin Jarre. A contemporary homage to the phrase can be found in the multi-player, first-shooter game *Overwatch*.

This is a roundabout way of putting a little meat on the bones of this story about Idaho's state fruit, the huckleberry. *What else is there to say about huckleberries, except, "Yum"?*

That luscious taste aside, huckleberry is a funny name. The friendly ghosts at Wikipedia tell us the name is "a North American variation of the English dialectal name variously called 'hurtleberry' or 'whortleberry,'" as if that explains anything. Huckle, hurtle, whortle, or whatever you'd like to call it, the berry became Idaho's official state fruit in 2000 when the combined fourth and fifth-grade class at Southside Elementary in Cocolalla convinced their legislators to introduce a bill to that effect. Cocolalla, Idaho is on Cocolalla Lake, about thirteen miles south of Sandpoint, close to the heart of huckleberry country. So, if you were hankering for Idaho's state fruit and wanted a personal guide to the best picking area, you could ask about any of the residents if they would be your huckleberry. Chances are good they wouldn't strike you, but you'll get some raised eyebrows. Also, they will not tell you where to pick.

THE CORPS OF DISCOVERY DISCOVERED THIS IDAHO SYMBOL

The Lewis and Clark expedition discovered not only Idaho but the Idaho state flower. In 1806, Captain Meriwether Lewis discovered and collected the first specimen of syringa. The shrub's scientific name, *Philadelphus lewisii*, recognizes that fact.

Of course, the plant wasn't new to the Indians. They had used it for generations, making soap from the leaves and arrows from the stems.

Syringa is a beautiful plant. The shrub grows from three to twelve feet high and features large clusters of white flowers with bright yellow stamens. A hillside covered with syringa in the spring can look almost like a snowfield. It would be hard to miss a big patch of the plant, even blindfolded. Syringa gives off a strong orange aroma. Many people call it mock orange.

You'll find syringa growing along streams and on hillsides to nearly 7,000 feet. It often grows along with chokecherry and serviceberry. One indicator of a large deer population is a stand of syringa that has been heavily browsed because the animals normally prefer other foods.

Another likely candidate for the honor of state flower might have been Clarkia, which is in the primrose family. Captain William Clark discovered it along Idaho's Clearwater River. Syringa became Idaho's state flower in 1931.

Syringa plant photo from the Idaho Department of Fish and Game public information web pages about Idaho species. Photo by Ryan Batten, 2011 (NC-SA 3.0).

A PERFECT MATCH

This Idaho state symbol is probably in your kitchen cupboard right now. The western white pine is an important tree for the timber industry. It's a durable, close-grained tree that is uniform in texture. It was named the state tree of Idaho by the 1935 Legislature.

White pine is lightweight, seasons without warping takes nails without splitting, and saws easily. That makes it a terrific tree for door and window frames, cabinets, and paneling. Oh yes, about the white pine that's in your cupboard right now—kitchen matches.

The western white pine does best in a cool and dry climate. Although it can grow at sea level, it prefers elevations of 2500 to 6000 feet. In Idaho, it grows mostly in the panhandle. A mature tree typically gets to be about 100 feet high.

A gregarious tree, the western white pine seems to prefer mixing with other common evergreens rather than in large stands of its own. One plant it would be better off not mixing with is the currant. A fungus called pine blister rust kills the pine, but it's only found where currants or gooseberries grow.

This photo is labeled as the "Largest Known White Pine" at 207 feet tall with a 6' 7" diameter. It scaled at 29,800 board feet measure. Its ring count shows it was 425 years old when cut down in 1912. The live tree was located seven miles northwest of Bovill. Photo courtesy of the Idaho State Historical Society, 78-37-158.

ORYCTODROMEUS

Idaho's newest state symbol is also its oldest. Designated as Idaho's State Dinosaur in 2023, *Oryctodromeus* lived about 98 million years ago during the Cretaceous Period. That makes Idaho's State Fossil, the Hagerman Horse, a relative newcomer, having lived here about 3.5 million years ago.

Paleontologist Dr. L. J. Krumenacker, an instructor at the College of Eastern Idaho, found the first fossilized remains of Oryctodromeus in the Caribou-Targhee National Forest in 2006. It was a lucky find since dinosaur fossils are rare in Idaho. Even so, Oryctodromeus is the most common dinosaur in the state.

Oryctodromeus was a burrowing dinosaur, so far the first to be discovered in the world. Oryctodromeus means "digging runner." They would have been good at both. The herbivore's burrows were large since the dinosaurs stood about three feet tall, weighed between fifty and seventy pounds, and were nearly eleven feet long. Most of that length—about two-thirds of it—was made up of a tail.

White Pine Charter School students in Ammon convinced lawmakers to add Oryctodromeus to the state's list of symbols. So far, fossils of this dinosaur have been found only in eastern Idaho and the southwest corner of Montana.

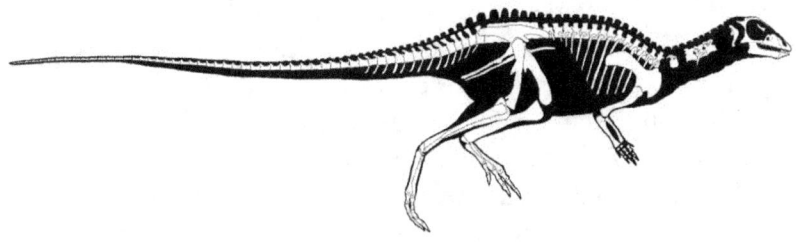

MORLEY NELSON AND IDAHO'S STATE RAPTOR

Idaho is a mecca for raptor lovers from all over the world. That's because it is a magnet for birds of prey. The World Center for Birds of Prey is in Boise. Boise State University is home to the Raptor Research Center and offers the only Master of Science in Raptor Biology, and The Morley Nelson Snake River Birds of Prey National Conservation Area (NCA) is south of Kuna.

The birds congregate in the NCA not because it is a protected area, but because it is an ideal place for raptors to live. The uplift of air from the Snake River Canyon makes flying and gliding a breeze for the birds. The uplands above the canyon rim provide a habitat for ground squirrels and other critters the birds consider lunch.

Morley Nelson first saw the canyon in the late 1940s. He had developed a love for raptors—especially peregrine falcons—growing up on a farm in North Dakota. When he moved to Idaho, following a WWII stint with the famous Tenth Mountain Division, he went out to the Snake River Canyon to see if he could find some raptors. He found a few. There are typically about 800 pairs of hawks, eagles, owls, and falcons that nest there each spring. It's the greatest concentration of nesting raptors in North America, and probably the world.

Nelson became evangelical about the birds and their Snake River Canyon habitat. He worked on films about the birds with Walt Disney, Paramount Pictures, the Public Broadcasting System, and others. His passion for raptors was contagious, and through his efforts, public understanding of their role in the natural world was greatly enhanced. Morley Nelson convinced Secretary of the Interior Rogers Morton to establish the Snake River Birds of Prey Natural area in 1971. He lobbied Interior Secretary Cecil Andrus to expand the area in 1980. Then in 1993, US Representative Larry LaRocco

THE IDAHO CONVERSION KIT

led an effort in Congress to designate some 485,000 acres of the canyon and uplands as a National Conservation Area.

It was also Nelson who led the effort to convince the Peregrine Fund to relocate to Boise and build the World Center for Birds of Prey south of town. Today, peregrines have recovered thanks to the center's captive breeding program and other efforts. The World Center for Birds of Prey now concentrates on programs to save the aplomado falcon and the California condor.

While efforts to recover peregrines were going on, Nelson led a pioneering effort to save raptors from power line electrocution. He worked with the Edison Electric Institute and Idaho Power to study how raptors used the man-made perches known as power poles. Because of that research, poles are now designed to minimize electrocution and even provide safe nesting areas for the birds.

Morley lived to see Idaho become the only state to have a state raptor. Thanks to the hard work of a group of fourth graders, the peregrine falcon became the state raptor in 2004.

When Morley Nelson passed away in 2005, he had unquestionably done more to save and protect raptors than any other single person.

For more on Morley Nelson, see his biography, *Cool North Wind: Morely Nelson's Life with Birds of Prey*, written by Steve Stuebner.

Morley Nelson with one of his favorite birds, a gyrfalcon named Thor. Photo courtesy of Stephen Stuebner.

DO SI DO

Our state's claim to the "Hokey Pokey" aside (see my Speaking of Idaho History Series book #1, *Symbols, Signs and Songs*, page 86), the dance was snubbed when in 1989 the Legislature declared Idaho's official state dance the square dance. It came out of the Senate Commerce and Labor Committee with a "Do Pass—with enthusiasm!" recommendation.

The National Folk-Dance Committee tried to make the square dance the official national dance in 1988, without success. As often happens when something fails on the national level, the group aimed their sites at the states. Idaho couldn't resist the lobbyists from Big Dance. It became one of nineteen states to decide, suddenly, that it just had to have a state dance.

I dance only in the shower, so have not participated in this particular passion. I am told that the name comes from the beginning placement of couples. Two face each other, let's say, north and south, and two east and west. In the American version of the dance, a caller calls out instructions to the dancers while the music plays. Apparently, without revulsion, the couples do-si-do on command. The square dance has its roots in sixteenth-century England, though it has become strongly associated with Western—as in cowboy Western—culture.

When the bill to make it the state dance was introduced, Idaho Senator Claire Wetherell, (D for Democrat and Dance) said, "Square dancing is typical of Idaho's lifestyle." Well, okay. I'm not sure I can get seven other people in the shower, though.

The Hokey Pokey was also known as Hokey Cokey in the UK, Australia, and Caribbean. Photo courtesy Wikipedia, Bryan Ledgard.

A SONG WITH A HISTORY

In 1915, Sallie Hume Douglas entitled her composition "Garden of Paradise." Over the years, at least four people have taken credit for writing lyrics to that music. With various combinations of verse and chorus, "Garden of Paradise" was called "Our Idaho," "Old Idaho," and finally "Here We Have Idaho," our state song. It's a song that has grown and changed and even went through a period of what you might call juvenile delinquency.

Before it became the state song, "Here We Have Idaho" was the school song of the University of Idaho. They called it "Our Idaho" or "Old Idaho." At that time, there was some question over which was the official version and who wrote the lyrics.

No one knew who wrote the music. No one, that is, except the composer who discovered her song was being used without permission. She threatened to sue the University of Idaho, and in 1930, they reluctantly purchased rights to the song. In 1931, "Here We Have Idaho" became the state song.

Over the years, there were many arguments over adaptations of the lyrics. The composer of the music threatened another lawsuit.

And Idahoans just went on singing of Idaho.

"Garden of Paradise," composed by Sallie Hume Douglas in 1915.

AN ART CONTEST WE STILL REMEMBER

The great seal of the State of Idaho was approved in 1891 and can be found on business cards, letterheads, brochures, proclamations, and other official state documents. It is also the centerpiece of Idaho's flag.

Emma Edwards Green, who was born in California and was the daughter of a former governor of Missouri, was teaching art classes in Boise when the brand-new Idaho Legislature announced a contest to design a state seal. She entered the competition and won 100 dollars. To this day, it remains the only state seal designed by a woman. Green got much input regarding the seal. She wrote,

> "Before designing the seal, I was careful to make a thorough study of the resources and future possibilities of the State. I invited the advice and counsel of every member of the Legislature and other citizens qualified to help in creating a Seal of State that really represented Idaho at that time."

Green also gave it a lot of thought, writing the following:

> The question of Woman Suffrage was being agitated somewhat, and as leading men and politicians agreed that Idaho would eventually give women the right to vote, and as mining was the chief industry, and the mining man the largest financial factor of the state at that time, I made the figure of the man the most prominent in the design, while that of the woman, signifying justice, as noted by the scales; liberty, as denoted by the liberty cap on the end of the spear, and equality with man as denoted by her position at his side, also signifies freedom. The pick and shovel held by the

miner, and the ledge of rock beside which he stands, as well as the pieces of ore scattered about his feet, all indicate the chief occupation of the State. The stamp mill in the distance, which you can see by using a magnifying glass, is also typical of the mining interest of Idaho. The shield between the man and woman is emblematic of the protection they unite in giving the state. The large fir or pine tree in the foreground in the shield refers to Idaho's immense timber interests. The husbandman plowing on the left side of the shield, together with the sheaf of grain beneath the shield, are emblematic of Idaho's agricultural resources, while the cornucopias, or horns of plenty, refer to the horticultural. Idaho has a game law, which protects the elk and moose. The elk's head, therefore, rises above the shield. The state flower, the wild Syringa or Mock Orange, grows at the woman's feet, while the ripened wheat grows as high as her shoulder. The star signifies a new light in the galaxy of states . . . The river depicted in the shield is our mighty Snake or Shoshone River, a stream of great majesty.

In regard to the coloring of the emblems used in the making of the Great Seal of the State of Idaho, my principal desire was to use such colors as would typify pure Americanism and the history of the State. As Idaho was a virgin state, I robed my goddess in white and made the liberty cap on the end of the spear the same color. In representing the miner, I gave him the garb of the period suggested by such mining authorities as former United States Senator George Shoup, of Idaho, former Governor Norman B. Willey of Idaho, former Governor James H. Hawley of Idaho, and other mining men and early residents of the state who knew intimately the usual garb of the miner. Almost unanimously they said,

"Do not put the miner in a red shirt. Make the shirt a grayish brown," said Captain J.J. Wells, chairman of the Seal Committee. The "Light of the Mountains" is typified by the rosy glow which precedes the sunrise.

If that sounds a little busy to you, you would not be alone. The state seal was updated in 1957 to simplify it a bit, though it remains, let's say, hard-working.

The $100 she won for designing Idaho's state seal did not make Emma Edwards Green wealthy, but it did bring her a measure of lasting fame. She is the only woman to have designed a state seal.

Amidst marble floors, steps, and columns, a beautiful mosaic of the Idaho state seal adorns the floor in the lowest level of the Statehouse. The mosaic contains 9,750 tiles that were hand laid and leveled onto the floor. Photo by Meggan Laxalt Mackey.

STEP 5
IDAHO SUPERLATIVES

The US Forest Service claims that Hells Canyon is the deepest gorge in North America, "carved by the great Snake River." The Hells Canyon National Recreation Area website also notes that there are no roads across Hells Canyon's 10-mile wide expanse, with only three roads that lead to the Snake River between Hells Canyon Dam and the Oregon-Washington border. Information and photo courtesy USDA Forest Service, Wallowa-Whitman Places pages.

SUPERLATIVES

What this country needs is more arguing, said nobody in the past six months. Nevertheless, this piece will probably start a few arguments.

Superlatives fascinate us if the *Guinness Book of World Records* is any indication. We want to know the biggest, the smallest, the widest, the most . . . and we certainly want to know the deepest.

CANYONS

One of Idaho's claims to fame is having the deepest canyon in North America. When measured from the top of He Devil Mountain to the splashing Snake River, Hells Canyon is 7,993 feet deep. At least, that's the number given most often.

But is that the deepest? Some folks claim that Kings Canyon in California is the deepest, at 8,200 feet. At a glance, Kings Canyon looks like the easy winner. *But how does one measure a canyon?* When you think of a canyon, your mind probably goes to Grand Canyon, with its sheer cliffs and brilliant colors. Now THAT'S a canyon! Yet, Grand Canyon, at its deepest, is only about 6,000 feet. There's no real issue about measuring the Grand Canyon. You might be able to use a plumb bob in spots and more than a mile of string, dropping it straight down. You couldn't do that at Hells Canyon because the point you measure from is the highest point in the Seven Devils Range, which is more than five miles from the river as the eagle flies.

In California, Spanish Mountain is 8,200 feet above the confluence of the King River's Middle and South forks, which is less than five miles away. A plumb bob wouldn't work there, either.

Now, I know they don't use a string and a weight to determine the difference in elevation between a river and the top of a peak. I use the plumb bob image just to make a point. That point is a question. *What is a canyon? Does a gorge count as a gorge if only one side has high cliffs?* If an asymmetrical canyon is okay with you, then Kings Canyon is probably your favorite for the deepest gorge. The mountains across from Spanish Mountain are a stubby 2,200 feet above the river.

Meanwhile, back in Idaho, the mountains on the Oregon side of the Snake are more than a mile above the river. That seems more gorge-like to me.

Hells Canyon wins on the internet, with most sites listing it as the deepest. *Wikipedia* calls it the deepest in North America at 7,933 feet, while mentioning in passing on the Kings Canyon page that it is "one of the deepest in North America" at 8,200 feet.

To muddy the canyon waters a bit further, some sites claim that Copper Canyon in Mexico is the deepest in North America, though with no substantiation.

Discuss amongst yourselves.

GLACIERS

On the north face of Idaho's highest peak, Mt. Borah (12,662 feet), and shaded nearly completely by that mountain rests a glacier of about twenty-five acres. A Boise State University geology student, Bruce Otto discovered it in 1975. Some have called the mountain cirque glacier Otto Glacier in honor of the man who discovered it.

With climate change on everyone's mind in recent years, there was speculation that the glacier had melted away. But two teams, one consisting of members of the Sloan family led by Collin Sloan and the other consisting of US Forest Service employees, trekked to the glacier in 2017 and found that it was largely still intact.

How could climbers have missed a twenty-five-acre glacier during all the years that people have been hiking to the top? Well, about two-thirds of the glacier is perpetually covered with rock debris. Glimpsing a cirque with a snowbank isn't unusual at most times of the year. No one had taken the trouble to climb down to that perpetual patch of white to determine if it was a glacier until 1975.

So, what makes a patch of snow and ice a glacier? According to the report (take a deep breath here) *The Otto Glacier on Borah Peak, Lost River Range, Custer County, Idaho: Reconnaissance Survey Finds Further Evidence for Active Glacier Watershed Monitoring Program,* "A glacier is defined as a perennial mass of land ice formed by the recrystallization of snow that accumulates stress leading to the downslope or outward motion of the ice mass." A couple of important terms there are "perennial" and "motion." Measurements using Google Earth imagery over three years concluded that the glacier moves downslope between 50 and 200 cm per year.

I should mention that the authors of the above-referenced paper were Joshua Keeley and Mathew Warbitton.

There are countless shaded spots in Idaho mountains above 10,000 feet where one can find ice year-round. Most aren't glaciers. Another type of glacier that doesn't fit the definition above, are rock glaciers. Rock glaciers are boulders fields with ice occupying the spaces between them, but the deposits don't grow enough to cause the whole mass to move. Glaciers move slowly, so barring a major meltdown, they don't make the news very often. One need not be fleet-footed to get out of their way.

The glacier on Borah Peak made a little news in 2021. Idaho was distinguished as one of the states without a named glacier. Sure, Florida and Kansas are in that category, too, but Idaho has a glacier. It just wasn't named. Note that I mentioned this one was sometimes called Otto Glacier. It might have been an excellent honor for Mr. Otto to have a glacier named after him, but one must be dead before a geographical feature can honor one. Bruce Otto is probably not eager to meet that requirement.

Who makes up these rules? Someone has to, or there would be chaos in cartographic circles. The U.S. Geographical Names Board (USGNB) is the entity that decides what name is official and should go on maps.

A proposal to name the feature the Borah Glacier recently went before the Idaho Geographical Names Advisory Council (IGNAC). The council recommended that the name Borah Glacier be placed on that icy feature. That recommendation went before the Idaho State Historical Society Board of Directors. They approved the recommendation, and *voila*, Idaho officially had a glacier.

THE IDAHO CONVERSION KIT

GOING BANANAS IN SUN VALLEY: THE FIRST DESTINATION SKI RESORT IN THE U.S.

Averell Harriman famously built the Sun Valley Ski Resort while he was the head of the Union Pacific Railroad as a way to get wealthy travelers to buy tickets on his trains. Built in 1936, it was the first winter destination resort in the U.S.

But Sun Valley boasts another first, even more important to skiers. A Union Pacific engineer named James Curran designed and installed the first chairlift at the mountain resort. It is important to note that

James Curran tested his early chairlifts for the Sun Valley Ski Resort miles away from the Idaho mountains—in the Union Pacific rail yards in Omaha, Nebraska. According to a story in the Smithsonian Magazine, *("Innovation: The Invention of the Ski Chairlift," February 2, 2021, by Sarah Kuta), a photo of Curran's rail yard testing hangs in the Sun Valley Lodge today. Photo courtesy The Community Library.*

in this case, "Union Pacific engineer" does not imply a man who operated locomotives.

Curran had developed a conveyor system to load bananas onto ships. He used what he learned on that project to build the first ski lifts on Proctor and Dollar mountains. The photo shows the testing of an early prototype.

Averell Harriman deserves credit for the resort, but it's Curran who gets credit for the first ski lift. James Curran was inducted into the National Ski Hall of Fame in 2001.

FLOODS

Our big state has some good-natured competition between the north and south. *Who has the best state parks? The best hunting and best fishing? The craziest politicians?*

Bragging rights for one thing are really no contest. The Bonneville Flood, which roared through what is now southern Idaho about 12,000 years ago was a monster. When ancient Lake Bonneville, which covered most of what is now Utah, broke through a natural plug at Red Rock Pass it sent water crashing down the channel of the Snake River five or six times the flow of the Amazon, tearing out chunks of canyon the size of cars and tumbling the rock into rounded boulders. It drained some 600 cubic miles of water into the Columbia and out to the Pacific in a matter of weeks and is said to be the second-biggest flood in geologic history.

Second biggest. *So, who had the first?* Northern Idaho, of course.

About 15,000 years ago, during the last ice age, a huge glacier blocked the flow of the Clark Fork River near where it enters Lake

Pend Oreille. Water backed up into present-day Montana, forming an expansive lake that geologists call Lake Missoula. The glacial lake covered 3,000 square miles, with a depth of up to 2,000 feet.

The ice dam that created Lake Missoula could not contain it forever. When the ice finally gave way—perhaps in the period of a day or two—a massive flood resulted.

You could not have outrun the rush of water called the Spokane Flood. It came ripping out of Idaho and into Washington at up to eighty miles per hour with the force of 500 cubic miles of water behind it. The flow may have run at 13 times the output of the Amazon. It's no wonder it scoured out 200-foot-deep canyons and ripped the topsoil away across 15,000 square miles of what is now Washington State.

So a couple of very big floods. Wait, more than that. The Bonneville Flood happened only once, while the Spokane Flood may have happened again and again—maybe up to 25 times—while ice dams formed and broke away.

Stay dry.

RIVERS

Idaho's Bear River holds a few superlative distinctions. First, though it is probably not unique in this sense, the Bear River flows through three states, Utah, Wyoming, and Idaho. It starts in Utah, winds into Wyoming, drifts back into Utah, then into Wyoming again before entering Idaho. The longest stretch of the river is in Idaho, looping up past Montpelier to Soda Springs, then plunging down and back into Utah, where it flows into the Great Salt Lake.

That's where it's one true superlative comes from. The Bear River is the largest in the United States, whose waters never reach an ocean. The outflow of the river is less than 100 miles from where it began, but the water journeys some 350 miles to get there.

It wasn't always so. The Bear River once—geologically once—flowed into the Snake River like most other respectable streams in southern Idaho. Lava flows that occurred long before you were born—maybe before anyone was born—diverted the flow south from Soda Springs.

The Bear River Canyon (image c. 1869). Image courtesy Wikipedia.

STEP 6
LAKE MONSTERS

Sharlie the Payette Lake Monster dances in the streets at the 2015 Winter Carnival in McCall, Idaho. Photo courtesy Visit McCall, McCall Chamber of Commerce publicity photo.

THE PAYETTE LAKE MONSTER

No self-respecting lake monster should go without a name. At least, that's what A. Boon McCallum, editor and publisher of the *Payette Lakes Star* thought.

Sightings of some sort of creature that seemed out of place in Payette Lake had been going on for years. The newspaper in McCall decided to run a contest in 1954 to give the poor beast a name. More than 200 people entered the contest. The suggestions ranged from the pseudo-scientific to variations on monster names. They included:

Boon
Fantasy
Nobby Dick
Humpy
Watzit
McFlash
High Ho
Peekaboo
Snorky
Neptune Ned
 . . . and on and on.
The winner, as you may know, was *Sharlie*.

Le Isle Hennefer Tury of Springfield, Virginia, walked away with the $40 prize for that one. Lest Idahoans grump too much about an out-of-stater winning the contest, it was pointed out that she had at one time lived in Twin Falls. I confess to having my own "Sharlie" sighting once while standing atop Porcupine Point in Ponderosa State Park. With no boats in sight for miles, the water below in The Narrows started churning. It continued to churn for about two minutes. There was no creepy music accompanying the phenomenon, so I just chalked it up to space aliens.

THE BEAR LAKE MONSTER

The first reports of the Bear Lake Monster were in a Salt Lake City newspaper in 1868. The paper printed stories from reporters in southeastern Idaho. Joseph C. Rich often wrote from the Idaho side of Bear Lake. Part of Bear Lake is in Idaho, and part is in Utah.

Rich told of Indian legends of a snake-like monster that had short, stubby legs. It would sometimes scurry onto shore and snatch away maidens in its terrible jaws.

But it wasn't just a legend. Rich wrote of people who saw the monster that very year. Just three weeks earlier one saw "two or three feet of some kind of an animal that he had never seen before raised out of the water." It had ears on the side of its head the size of "a pint cup."

Then a man and three women saw something very large swimming in the lake faster than a horse could run.

A few days later three men saw a beast they said was ninety feet long. One of them said he had never seen a train go that fast. Then they spotted a second, smaller monster. This one was only forty feet long.

Rich reported that "the waves that rolled up in front and on each side of them" were three feet high.

Readers wrote to the paper with ideas about the monsters. One thought sea lions got stranded in the lake when an ancient ocean dried up. Others thought fossils held a clue. Maybe the monster was a swimming dinosaur.

Several people said they, too, saw the monster. Many scoffed at the stories. J.C. Rich wrote how sorry he was for unbelievers. "They might come up here someday, and through their unbelief, be thrown off their guard and gobbled up by the Water Devil."

THE IDAHO CONVERSION KIT

Rich often wrote tongue-in-cheek. The story about the Bear Lake monster was part of a longer article. It started this way: "It is a mystery to me that all the leading journals of the world have not correspondents in Bear Lake. In fact, I don't know how the people tolerate their publications without."

He went on to describe the styles in Paris. Paris, Idaho. Those included "cow sheds and other items." He also told of invading grasshoppers "well disciplined, armed, and equipped for war."

The monster sightings went on even after 1888. That was when the reporter finally admitted he made the whole thing up. *Why?* Just for fun. The fact he owned a resort on Bear Lake may have played a part. The publicity was great! Even today people claim they have seen the "monster." That would have amused the father of the monster, Joseph C. Rich.

The most famous folklore monster is Scotland's Loch Ness Monster, also called "Nessie." Historical illustration sketched by A. Grant from Lieut.-Commander Gould's monograph about the Loch Ness Monster (date unknown). Courtesy Wikipedia.

STEP 7
NICKNAMES

Richard "Beaver Dick" Leigh

BEAVER DICK

Richard "Beaver Dick" Leigh, born in Manchester, England in 1831, came to what would become Idaho in the late 1840s. Leigh was a mountain man in the waning days of the fur trade, thus his self-imposed nickname, picked for his proficiency in catching the rodents.

There are a lot of stories about Richard Leigh. A few bullet points:

• When the Hayden Expedition needed a guide for their famous exploration of Yellowstone country, it was Beaver Dick they chose.

• Leigh Lake in Grand Teton National Park is named after him. Nearby Jenny Lake is named after his first wife.

• Beaver Dick lost his entire first family, his wife Jenny and their four kids, to smallpox.

• Leigh helped a Shoshoni woman give birth to a daughter, Susan, who was promised to become Beaver Dick's wife. He didn't think it would ever happen, but they did marry sixteen years later after Leigh lost his first family.

• He may be the only historical figure to have two Idaho highway historical markers, one near Rexburg and the other in Boise.

• Leigh is far better known in Eastern Idaho where he lived most of his life, but the second historical marker for Beaver Dick is located not far from Boise's Idaho Shakespeare Festival theater. For the best account of that brief period in his life, we turn to the diary of Charles Teeter.

• In 1863, Teeter wrote, "We were the first to cross the [Boise] river on a new ferry just constructed by an old mountaineer called Beaver Dick, consequently the ferry was to bear that name. Beaver Dick himself, accompanied by two or three of his men, brought over the ferry boat, and we were soon safely landed on the other side. Here we spent the night and as Beaver Dick was the first man we had seen who had visited the Boise gold mines, we had many questions to ask concerning them."

• It's worth noting that the "old mountaineer" was 32 at the time. Living rough ages one, apparently.

• Beaver Dick's Ferry operated in 1863 and 1864 near where the Crow Inn was for many years on Warm Springs Boulevard, just west of Highway 21. The historical marker at the site says the following:
"In 1863 and 1864, overland packers hauling supplies from Salt Lake City to Idaho City crossed here and took a direct route northward to More's Creek.

"They cut a steep grade from the Oregon Trail down to Beaver Dick's Ferry, which served as a crossing only a short distance below here. After gold rush excitement ended, Idaho City traffic came on through Boise and used a toll road further north to Boise Basin."

BUCKSKIN BILL

Idaho has long sent a siren song to people who want to escape the world. "Buckskin Bill," sometimes called the "Last of the Mountain Men," may be the best known.

We associate mountain men with the fur-trapping era of the 1800s. Sylvan Hart, who became known as "Buckskin Bill," turned into a man of the mountains nearly a century later in 1932. He started his adventure as a way to ride out the depression. He stayed for the rest of his life.

Hart believed in education. He attended four colleges, getting a B.A. in English Literature from the University of Oklahoma. For his continuing education, he became a hermit living on the banks of the Salmon River. In Cort Conley's excellent book, *Idaho Loners*, he quotes Hart as saying, "I wasn't trying to run away from anything. I was just a natural born student, and I could study there, investigate for myself, and I could experiment with different things. I'm not going to give up on education. It doesn't pay to stop. Once you get really dumb, there's no redemption for you."

Hart, along with his father, Artie, picked a spot on Five Mile Bar to live off the land. Artie eventually had enough of the Salmon River Country and moved into town. Sylvan stayed on, winter after long winter, spending six months at a time without seeing a soul.

"Buckskin Bill" tended a large garden, hunted, and panned a little gold for his living. He got his name from Don Oberbillig, who lived at Mackay Bar three miles down the river. Buckskin was what Hart wore. Where "Bill" came from is not exactly clear. Alliteration probably played a part.

Hermits are famously drop-outs from society. Hart ran against type in that respect. When he heard about Pearl Harbor, a few months after the event, he hiked out to Grangeville to join the

Army. They wouldn't have him because of an enlarged heart and because at 35, he was a little old for the front lines.

Hart still wanted to help in the war effort. He got himself to Wichita, Kansas where he took a job as a toolmaker with Boeing.

In 1942, with the war roaring, the Army lowered its standards for inductees. They inducted Sylvan Hart and posted him to Amchitka in the Aleutian Islands. The Japanese had taken over the remote territory. Hart's group was meant to oust them, but they left before he saw any action. Oddly, the FBI had been looking for him, thinking he was a draft dodger.

The Army sent Hart to Colorado, where he helped develop a top-secret bombsight.

Shortly after the war ended, he drifted back to his home in Idaho. Back to gardening, hunting, fishing, and making. He made everything he used, from kitchen utensils to guns. His flintlock rifles, which took a year to make, were hand-rifled and hand-bored, with elaborately carved wooden stocks.

Buckskin Bill's brush with the FBI was a mistake. His brush with the IRS was purposeful bureaucracy. He didn't care much for money. Many of his checks from his Army days went uncashed for so long that they expired. He didn't feel an obligation to pay taxes since, by his estimation, he didn't make $500 a year. The IRS had a different math. They sent him threatening letters because of his lack of filings. So, Sylvan Hart turned himself in, arriving in Boise in full "Buckskin Bill" regalia.

Hart set up camp in the IRS office. He rolled out his sleeping bag on the floor and brewed a pot of tea. A supervisor was summoned. Bill offered him a cup of tea. He explained to the IRS that he was ready to go to prison if need be. He had brought along a supply of pemmican for his stay. Recognizing that this wasn't your average tax scofflaw, IRS officials sent him back to Five Mile Bar and never bothered him again.

THE IDAHO CONVERSION KIT

But the world wouldn't leave Buckskin Bill alone. In 1966, a writer for *Sports Illustrated* showed up on his doorstep. The resulting article, titled, "The Last of the Mountain Men," assured that Buckskin Bill would never be anonymous again. An expanded version of the story came out in book form a few years later.

This new-found fame didn't bother Sylvan Hart, the sometimes hermit. He loved to regale rafters and hikers with stories about his life in the Salmon River Country. Buckskin Bill became a celebrity of the backcountry, enjoying his solitude and fame in equal measures.

In 1980, Buckskin Bill passed away, making it just shy of 74 years. Friends conducted his funeral in Grangeville, then flew his body to Mackay Bar to be hauled upriver by boat. He was interred on his Five Mile Bar property, which remains a popular spot for rafters to visit today.

Buckskin Bill, also known as "The Last of the Mountain Men," c. 1974. Photo courtesy Alamy Images: https://www.alamy.com/buckskin-bill, Image #425555544.

DIAMOND TOOTH LIL

First, let's concede that at least a couple of women went by the name of "Diamond Tooth Lil." One, real name Honora Ornstein, was a vaudeville performer well-known in the Klondike Gold Rush days. Her affectation of diamonds included much jewelry and several gold teeth studded with diamonds.

Idaho's Diamond Tooth Lil was an entertainer and entrepreneur who bounced around the West from Silver City to San Francisco, spending significant time in Boise as a manager of rooming houses which were rumored to offer unadvertised recreational activities. Her birth name was Evelyn Fialla (some sources say Prado was her last name), and she was born in Austria-Hungary in about 1877. She married at least eight times, but the name she preferred to use was her first husband's surname, Hildegard. Everyone else preferred *Diamond Tooth Lil*.

Lil loved to tell the story of her life to any reporter who would listen. She often talked about her gold left front tooth with the diamond, about 1/3 carat, mounted in the center of it. She won that piece of art from a Reno dentist in a bet on a horse race in 1907. More than once, she promised to leave the tooth and its diamond to the Idaho Children's Home orphanage. What finally happened to it is open to speculation.

Diamond Tooth Lil's stories were often about the love of her life, Diamondfield Jack. They spent time with each other over the years in Idaho and Nevada. She said he asked her to marry him many times, but she declined. They lost track of each other for 30 years but reunited briefly at a Las Vegas casino in 1946, and in Los Angeles shortly before his death.

When Diamondfield Jack was struck by a cab in 1946 at 84, it was Diamond Tooth Lil who alerted the *Idaho Statesman*. Before his death, she reported that he had exonerated the taxi driver, saying, "I just wasn't looking where I was going."

She ran an auto court called the Depot Inn on the bench near the Boise Depot and a hotel at 219 S. Ninth, among other Boise properties. She moved to Los Angeles to retire in 1943, but visited Boise regularly. In 1953, she sent photos and other items to the Boise Chamber of Commerce with a note, "Just sending a little momento (sic), so you'll not forget me."

There's little chance Diamond Tooth Lil will be forgotten. Mae West wrote a successful Broadway play called *Diamond Lil* in 1928, which was turned into a movie called *She Done Him Wrong* and was revived on Broadway in 1949. Many say it was inspired by one Diamond Tooth Lil or the other, or perhaps the pair of them.

There's that diamond! Look closely at this photo. You can't make out much, but she clearly has something going on with that top left front tooth. Photo courtesy of the Idaho State Archives photo collection.

DIAMONDFIELD JACK

He got his nickname from his belief that there was a diamond mine near Silver City in Owyhee County. Diamondfield Jack became a household name in Idaho for reasons that had nothing to do with mining, though.

Sheep are very efficient grazers. They're able to crop off grass right down to ground level. That doesn't leave a thing for cattle to eat, and that's why there were range wars in the West. In Idaho, this basic conflict resulted in the deaths of two sheepmen in Cassia County in 1896.

Diamondfield Jack was a gunman hired by cattlemen to intimidate sheepmen. He'd threatened all of them at one time or another, so it was natural to assume he was involved in the murders. The man was arrested, prosecuted, convicted, and sentenced to hang. But hanging Diamondfield Jack proved difficult. Frantic men on horseback twice galloped into Albion carrying postponements, saving him from the gallows at the last minute. The third time Jack was scheduled to hang, two cattlemen came forward and confessed to the murders. They were eventually acquitted on self-defense.

Even with a confession, tests that proved the murder weapon wasn't his gun, and an alibi that placed him in Nevada at the time of the murders, many were still convinced that Diamondfield Jack pulled the trigger.

Diamondfield Jack's booking photo.

There was enough opposition to keep him in jail for six years.

But eventually, Diamondfield Jack was released.

The man who was saved from the gallows three times moved to Nevada, where his luck finally ran out.

Diamondfield Jack, who lived at least part of his life by the gun, did not die that way. He was run over by a taxicab in Las Vegas in 1949.

There are several books available about Diamondfield Jack. One of the most interesting is *Diamondfield: Finding the Real Jack Davis*, by Max Black.

Jack had an infamous love, Diamond Tooth Lil.

DOC HISOM

Doc Hisom (or Hison, or Hyson, as some references have it), was born in about 1858, a free man in Illinois. In his later years, he seemed to delight in telling people he was a little older than he really was, so his birth year is uncertain. His marker in the Kohlerlawn Cemetery in Nampa, lists his birth date as October 6, 1850.

William C. Hisom came by his nickname legitimately. He had trained as a veterinarian and worked as one for some years before coming to Idaho to seek his fortune as a miner in the late 1800s. He, a Black man, partnered up with a white man named White. They claimed a twenty-acre parcel along the Snake River near Melba in 1906 or 1907. They worked their claim for a few years before White drifted away. Doc Hisom lived there for the rest of his life.

Hisom was well known in the area as a storyteller and for his proficiency in practicing Native American and pioneer skills, such as flint knapping and working leather. One reference mentioned that he had at least some Indian blood.

A man of any color living miles from anywhere by his own hand doesn't make the newspaper very often. I found just one story about him in the *Idaho Statesman*. It reported a big event in his life. In October of 1921, Doc Hisom made his way into Boise for the second time in thirty-six years. He marveled at the electric lights and the rapid transit of the city. The miner took his first ride on a streetcar and in an automobile during that trip.

The paper reported that the recluse was a friend of "Two-Gun Bob" Limbert, the man who almost single-handedly got Craters of the Moon named a national monument. Limbert often stayed at Hisom's cabin. They probably discussed photography, among other things since both were accomplished photographers. Taxidermy was a skill they also shared. Hisom may have entertained "Two-Gun Bob" by playing music for him. He could play seven instruments.

We don't know for certain when Doc Hisom was born, but we do know when he died. That was December 26, 1944.

"Doc" Hisom working leather at his cabin along the Snake River.

TWO-GUN BOB AND HIS DOG

Robert Limbert was a Renaissance man of the West. He was a taxidermist, a hunting guide, an exhibit designer, an explorer, a writer, a photographer, and a tireless promoter of Idaho. Limbert was known as "Two-Gun Bob" when he was demonstrating his shooting skills to an audience. He built Redfish Lake Lodge, and on and on.

Limbert was the man who explored what we now know as Craters of the Moon and wrote the 25-page article that appeared in *National Geographic* in 1924 that intrigued the nation enough for Calvin Coolidge to proclaim it a national monument later that year. The article is available online and includes many of Lambert's pictures that are still stunning today.

The *National Geographic* article documented a trip he and a friend took across the forbidding black desert. Here's the cavalier way he described it:
> "One morning in May W. L. Cole and I, both of Boise, Idaho, left Minidoka, packing on our backs bedding, an aluminum cook outfit, a 5x7 camera and tripod, binoculars, and supplies sufficient for two weeks, making a total pack each of fifty-five pounds."

And now, to an important footnote:
> "We also took with us an Airedale terrier for a camp dog. This was a mistake, for after three days' travel, his feet were worn raw and bleeding. In some places, it was necessary to carry him or sit and wait while he picked his way across."

The dog of the adventure was not named Scout, or Hercules, or Intrepid. He was named Teddy. He was mentioned once more in the article: "The dog was in terrible shape also: it was pitiful to watch him as he hobbled after us." Left at what Limbert wrote for *National Geographic* you might think he just watched his companion animal suffer. He did much more than that for the Airedale. He cut up clothing to make booties for the dog, then did it again when they wore out. The three of them—two men and a dog—covered 80 miles in 17 days.

Limbert was a tireless promoter of Idaho, and of Robert Limbert, for which we should be glad.

Top: A photo of a "lava spout in Vermilion Canyon" appeared in National Geographic *magazine, with Limbert, Limbert's dog Teddy, and May W. L Cole. Limbert was in most of the photos he took of the expedition, which apparently were shot using a timer or remote shutter release.*

Right: Robert Limbert with a horse and saddle. Photo from the Robert Limbert papers, courtesy of Boise State University, Albertsons Library, Special Collections and Archives (MSS 080, #11032).

DUGOUT DICK

Dick Zimmerman's story was in *National Geographic* and *Life Magazine*. He got an invitation to appear on Johnny Carson's *Tonight Show* and turned it down. His obituary was in the *Wall Street Journal. So how did Zimmerman end up getting all that publicity and more?* Well, for the latter, he had to die, but not just anyone who stops breathing makes the cut.

What Dick Zimmerman did was live in something like a cave alongside Idaho's Salmon River.

Zimmerman had ridden the rails for a few years, bouncing around the country and working odd jobs when, at age 32, he decided to become a hermit. There may be no better place to do that than Idaho. He picked a boulder-strewn slope along the Salmon River about 20 miles south of the town of Salmon.

He made himself a home by moving rocks around and forming boulder and shale walls tucked back into a rockslide with a log front. The four-room rock-sheltered house featured a natural refrigerator in the back, taking advantage of a vein of ice that had formed over the centuries beneath the talus slope.

Zimmerman decided to make a little money by building more dugouts in the rocks and renting them out to people who wanted the experience of sleeping in a cave in Idaho's backcountry. Against common sense, there was no shortage of such people.

Eventually, Zimmerman earned the name "Dugout Dick" for his twenty-some rental properties scattered up and down the hillside, none of which would likely make the grade for Airbnb. He used whatever building materials he could scrounge, old tires, worn-out carpeting, and pieces of siding from an abandoned trailer. Floors were often concrete overlaid with linoleum scraps. Each had a wood stove and a bed or two. For windows, he used scrap glass, even car windshields. The roofs were typically rough-cut logs topped with scraps of siding and carpeting and covered with sod. You could have the experience of sleeping in one of those hand-built dugouts for a couple of dollars a night, with a discount if you wanted to stay for 30 days.

Dugout Dick married once in 1968. He met his wife through a lonely-hearts club. They corresponded, got hitched, and she came to live with him along the Salmon. She didn't take to the life and eventually drifted away. Zimmerman later had a girlfriend from Idaho Falls, according to Cort Conley's book *Idaho Loners*. She spent time with Dick off and on but came to a sad ending, murdered by her roommate in town.

Dugout Dick was less of a hermit than one might suppose. He went to town regularly, traveled a little, and didn't live a life all that secluded. You could throw a rock from his home on the hillside across the river and nearly hit US 93. Still, his odd lifestyle made him famous. A Scandinavian company did a documentary about the man. The magazine stories drew the curious to his "caves." Dick's home, and the rentals he built, were on land under the purview of the Bureau of Land Management. While he was alive, they tolerated the ramshackle little town he had built on the hillside. After his death at age 94 in 2010, BLM took down all but one of his constructions. Today there is an interpretive sign near that old dugout.

Dugout Dick in front of a sign that advertised him as the "Salmon River Cave Man."

PEG LEG ANNIE

Annie McIntyre came to the gold camp of Rocky Bar on July 4th, 1864, and she came in a most unusual way.

Annie was just four years old, and she arrived in a backpack carried by her father. It was when she was 38 years old and had five children of her own that Annie—then Annie Morrow—experienced the tragedy that made her an Idaho legend.

In the late spring of 1898, she and a lady friend called Dutch Em decided to make a snowshoe trip from Atlanta over the mountains to Rocky Bar. A trip over the hump that late in the winter shouldn't have been a problem, but a howling snowstorm caught Annie and Dutch Em by surprise. The blizzard raged for three days.

When searchers found Annie, she was crawling through the snow, delirious, wearing only a thin covering of clothes. She had given almost all her clothing to Dutch Em, trying to keep her friend warm. It was a futile attempt. Dutch Em froze to death.

Annie survived the ordeal, but her feet were so badly frostbitten they had to be amputated. She was a fighter though, and the loss of her feet didn't slow her down much. Though friends made crude artificial limbs for her, Annie usually found it faster to get around by crawling.

For many years after that, Annie ran a restaurant and rooming house. The miners had a lot of respect for the tough Idaho lady they nicknamed Peg Leg Annie.

HELL'S BELLE

Born Gracie Bowers in 1906 in Harrison, Arkansas, no one would have predicted that she would one day get the nickname "Hell's Belle" while serving in the U.S. House of Representatives from Idaho's 1st Congressional District.

Gracie's family moved to an Idaho farm near Meridian when she was five. In 1922, she quit high school to take a job in Nampa as a milk analyst. A year later, Gracie married a man twice her age, Jack Pfost, who was her supervisor.

Though Gracie Pfost never graduated from high school, she did go on to get a degree from Links Business College. That helped her become deputy county clerk in Canyon County. She ran for auditor and won, and then ran for treasurer. She won that office, too, and became the biggest vote-getter, even though she was a Democrat in a Republican county.

The Democrats took notice of her ability to win votes across party lines and talked her into running for Congress in 1950. She lost. Then, in 1952, she ran again against Congressman John Travers Wood, narrowly defeating him. The first female member of Congress from Idaho, she was reelected in 1954, 1956, 1958, and 1960, winning by a bigger margin every time.

In the book *Conversations*, edited by Susan Stacy, Idaho Congressman Ralph Harding remembered how the Republicans put up the Mayor of Caldwell, Erwin Schweibert, to run against Pfost in 1960.

His campaign hammered on the theme that Idaho needed a strong, energetic man as a representative. While both were campaigning in North Idaho, Gracie challenged the strong, energetic man to a log-rolling contest during Lumber Jack Days. She sank his campaign when Gracie quickly dumped him into the river.

Pfost got the nickname "Hell's Belle" in her first year in Congress by aggressively advocating for a single high dam on the Snake River in Hells Canyon. Ultimately that proposal went down to defeat, replaced by the three-dam complex we have today, Brownlee, Oxbow, and Hells Canyon.

Pfost ran for Senate in 1962 against powerhouse Senator Len B. Jordan, losing the race narrowly. She worked for the Federal Housing Administration after leaving Congress. Gracie Pfost died in 1965 at the age of 59 from Hodgkin's disease.

JACKSON SUNDOWN

Did *you ever play cowboys and Indians as a kid?* This story is about a man who wasn't playing. He was a cowboy and an Indian.

Waaya-Tonah-Toesits-Kahn was a nephew of Nez Perce Chief Joseph. He was 14 in 1877 when the flight of the Nez Perce took place across much of Idaho and parts of Oregon, Wyoming, and Montana. His uncle famously surrendered with the eloquent "I will fight no more forever" speech at Bear Paws Battlefield in Montana.

Jackson Sundown, a Native American and Pendleton Round-Up icon, was inducted into the American Athletic Hall of Fame, the National Multicultural Western Heritage Museum and Hall of Fame, and the National Cowboy and Western Heritage Museum and Hall of Fame. Photo courtesy Pendleton Round-Up.

Meanwhile, Waaya-Tonah-Toesits-Kahn, wounded, went with a small group of Nez Perce into Canada where he lived for a couple of years with Sitting Bull's Sioux.

He lived in Washington and Montana, gaining a reputation as a skilled horseman, and a new name, Jackson Sundown, before moving to Idaho in 1910. His skills atop a bucking bronco became so well-known that other riders would simply pull out of the competition when they heard Sundown had signed up. At least one rodeo manager solved that problem by paying Sundown $50 a day for exhibition bronc riding.

In 1911, Sundown along with George Fletcher, who was black, and John Spain, a white cowboy, competed at the Pendleton (Oregon) Roundup in a famous multi-racial showdown. Ken Kesey told that story in his 1995 book, *Last Go Round*.

In 1915, at the age of 52, Jackson Sundown came in only third in bronc riding at the Pendleton Roundup. He decided to retire. But the next year, Alexander Phimister Proctor, a noted sculptor who was working on a sculpture of Sundown at the time talked the man into riding just once more. Jackson won the saddle bronc competition that day at the age of 53. Many of his competitors were half that age or less.

Jackson Sundown died of pneumonia in 1923. He was buried at Slickpoo Mission Cemetery near Culdesac, Idaho. He was inducted into the Cowboy Hall of Fame in 2006.

FEARLESS FARRIS

Farris Lind was a crop duster, but he didn't get his nickname, "Fearless," for flying the farms with the most dangerous turns. He just liked the alliteration when he heard about Fearless Fosdick. Lind also served as a WWII flight instructor.

He ran his first gas station in 1936 when he was only 20 years old. That one was in Twin Falls.

After returning from service in WWII, Lind thought up a way to make his Boise service station famous. He scattered humorous signs all over southern Idaho to perk up drivers bored with many miles of sagebrush. One side advertised his growing number of Stinker Stations, while the other side offered humor, such as, in a field of lava rock (melon gravel left over from the Bonneville Flood), "Petrified watermelon. Take one home to your mother-in-law."

During an Ad Club luncheon in Boise in 1948, Lind talked about his three pet skunks, Cleo, Theo, and B.O., and how often people told him they had pet skunks when they were kids, which led Lind to postulate that eighty percent of Boiseans had pet skunks at one time. He told stories about people who would stop in to talk about his signs, often bringing one of those petrified watermelons to him. One of his favorites was a sign that said, "No fishing within 400 yards." It was placed miles from any drop of water. Lind said people would stop a way down the road, turn around, and take another look. One guy allegedly walked half a mile down a dry wash looking for fishing country.

Lind got into the humorous sign business almost by accident. In 1946, with the war behind him, he tried to buy exterior plywood to advertise his service station, but only interior plywood was available. That meant both sides had to be painted to preserve the wood. Lind was quoted in the *Idaho Statesman*, saying, "As long as the back side of the sign was painted, I got the idea of putting humor or curiosity-catching remarks on the back side."

Some of those remarks include:
"Lava is free. Make your own soap."

"This area is for the birds. It's fowl territory."

"Nudist area. (Keep your eyes on the road.)"

"Sheepherders headed for town have right of way."

"For a fast pickup, pass a state patrolman."

At one time, there were about 150 Stinker Station signs between Green River, Wyoming, and Jordan Valley, Oregon. Farris Lind came up with the humor for every one of them.

THE IDAHO CONVERSION KIT

Lind contracted polio in 1963. He continued to run his company from an iron lung after that, never losing his trademark sense of humor.

He got a few complaints about his signs. Several people didn't cotton to his sign outside of Salt Lake City that declared, "Salt Lake City is full of lonely, beautiful women." To avoid offending anyone, he had the word "lonely" removed. A similar sign about the women near Glenns Ferry prompted someone to scrawl "Where?" across it.

One of my personal favorites is still standing near Beeches Corner in Idaho Falls. It says, "Warning to tourists: Do not laugh at the natives." About a billion years ago I was riding in a car with a fellow ten-year-old. He saw the sign and turned to me in wonder, asking, *"Are there NATIVES around here!?"*

Fearless Farris Lind passed away in 1983. My book about Farris Lind is called *Fearless*. It's available online and in local bookstores.

Edward Pangborn and his co-pilot Hugh Herndon sought to break the record for circumnavigating the globe in 1931. They flew their plane, Miss Veeedol, a Bellanca CH-400.

UPSIDE DOWN PANG

In about 1919, St. Maries, that north Idaho logging town on the banks of the Shadowy St. Joe, was the site of a portentous meeting between famous aviators. Neither had yet risen to fame, but Edward Pangborn was well on his way.

Pangborn, who grew up in St. Maries and took civil engineering courses at the University of Idaho for a couple of years, learned to fly during World War I, becoming a flight instructor at Ellington Field in Houston. He gained a reputation there for stunt flying, earning the nickname "Upside Down Pang."

It was stunt flying—barnstorming—that brought him back to St. Maries following the war. He was a pilot for Gates Flying Circus and a partner in the operation. As barnstorming pilots often did, Pangborn offered short flights to local citizens. Little Gregory Hallenbeck got his first ride in an airplane that day. He would later become a famous Medal of Honor winner during World War II (see following story).

Pangborn's fame grew during his nine years as a barnstormer. He was known particularly for changing planes in mid-air, walking out on the wing of one plane and slipping over to the wing of another, flying wingtip to wingtip.

In 1931, Pangborn and co-pilot Hugh Herndon sought to break the record for circumnavigating the globe. Nasty weather in Siberia caused them to abandon their efforts. So, they set their sights on another record. The two flew to Japan, where they hoped to win a $25,000 prize for being the first to complete a non-stop trans-Pacific flight.

Their attempt was plagued with problems. First, they were arrested for taking pictures while flying over Japanese naval installations. Paying a $1,000 fine got them released, but the

Japanese kicked them out of the country. They could take off, but they would be arrested again if they tried to land in Japan because they didn't have proper documentation.

One chance was all they needed. They filled their plane, a Bellanca CH-400 called Miss Veedol, with over 900 gallons of fuel and took off on October 4, 1931. The term "flying by the seat of their pants" may not have been invented to describe this flight, but that is largely what they had to do. Their maps and charts had been stolen by a group that wanted a Japanese pilot to be the first to cross the Pacific non-stop.

Part of the plan to get across the ocean with limited fuel was to drop the landing gear from the plane so there would be less drag. The wheels fell away when the lever inside the cockpit was pulled, but a pair of struts stubbornly remained in place. Those caused unwanted drag, which would use precious fuel and make a belly landing—their plan—dangerous. Harkening back to his wing-walking days, Pangborn slipped out of the cockpit at 14,000 feet, barefoot, and removed the struts manually.

Everything went swimmingly from then on except for their inability to land and that time when the engine quit because the co-pilot had neglected to transfer fuel from the auxiliary tanks to the main on time. The plane, stripped of everything not necessary, didn't have a starter. The aircraft also lacked survival gear, seat cushions, and a radio. Pangborn put the Bellanca into a nosedive to get the prop spinning fast enough to start the plane. We know that worked because I did not just write, "and then they died."

The weather was again their enemy, as it had been over Siberia during the global attempt. They planned to land in Seattle or Vancouver, B.C., but both airfields were socked in. So was Mt. Rainier, which they came close to kissing. So, on to Boise! But no, fog had Boise, Spokane, and Pasco closed.

THE IDAHO CONVERSION KIT

All they wanted to do, badly, was land. And, eventually, they did. Badly, one could say. Of course, given that the plane had no landing gear, any landing one could walk away from was perfect. Pangborn and Herndon belly-landed in the dirt field at Wenatchee forty-one hours and thirteen minutes after taking off from Japan, officially becoming the first to fly non-stop across the Pacific.

Trans-Pacific and trans-Atlantic flights would become routine for Pangborn, who joined the Royal Air Force (RAF) in 1939. He made 170 trans-oceanic flights in helping to recruit American pilots to the cause. When the U.S. entered the war in 1941, he signed up with the U.S. Army Air Force.

Pangborn passed away in 1958 and is buried at Arlington National Cemetery.

Gregory "Pappy" Boyington

PAPPY BOYINGTON

Gregory Hallenbeck was born in Coeur d'Alene in 1912, but at age three, he moved with his family to the logging town of St. Maries. It was there, at age six, that Gregory had his first airplane ride with barnstormer Clyde Pangborn. He would cruise the clouds many times after that.

The Hallenbeck family moved to Tacoma when he was twelve. Gregory attended the University of Washington, graduating in 1934 with a BS in aeronautical engineering. He married and went to work for Boeing as an engineer and draftsman.

Gregory wanted to fly, not just work on airplane design. In 1935, he applied for a slot with the Navy as an aviation cadet. They rejected him because he was married. He wasn't going to get a divorce, so that path into the air seemed closed. That is until he got a copy of his birth certificate and learned that Ellsworth Hallenback, his father, was not really his father. Gregory's father was a dentist by the name of Charles Boyington. Boyington and Gregory's mother had divorced when Gregory was a baby.

Finding out your personal history was not what you thought it was might have been traumatic for the young man, but Gregory changed his name to his birth name and reapplied to the Navy program. Under that new/old name, he didn't bother to mention that he was married. They accepted him as an aviation cadet.

In 1937, Gregory Boyington became a second lieutenant in the Marine Corps. Then in 1941, Boyington took what might have seemed to be a detour. He resigned his commission in the Marine Corps and went to work for the Central Aircraft Manufacturing Company. The company was real, but the job was a ruse.

American entrepreneur William Pawley ran the company in China. In 1941, he began recruiting pilots for his American Volunteer Group, also known as the "Flying Tigers. "President Franklin Roosevelt authorized the covert operation where the US pilots would fly airplanes marked with the colors of China, fighting the Japanese. Ironically, they didn't see their first action until 12 days after the attack on Pearl Harbor.

Boyington was credited with the destruction of three Japanese aircraft during his brief stint with the Flying Tigers, two in the air and one on the ground. In September 1942, he rejoined the Marine Corps, where his story would become legendary. A year later, he would become the commanding officer of Marine Fighter Squadron 214, nicknamed the Black Sheep Squadron.

It was while he was with the Black Sheep that he earned a nickname. They called him "Gramps" because at 31, he was years older than most of the pilots. That morphed into "Pappy," giving him the moniker that would stay with him in the history books, Gregory "Pappy" Boyington,

During his first tour, "Pappy" took down 14 enemy fighters in 32 days. He shared the bravura and a bit of the PR man with Pangborn, the barnstormer who first took him into the skies. Boyington and his men would buzz enemy airfields, luring fighters into the sky where they could be picked off. The PR man appeared when he boasted that he and his squadron would shoot down a Japanese Zero for every cap the ball players in the World Series would send them. They got 20 hats. The Japanese lost 20 aircraft and then some.

But his luck didn't hold. In January 1944, Boyington was shot down over the Pacific just after making his own twenty-sixth kill. He was presumed dead, but he had actually been plucked out of the water by

THE IDAHO CONVERSION KIT

a Japanese submarine. For nearly two years, Boyington was a POW, freed finally when American forces liberated the Omori Prison Camp.

For his wartime heroics, Gregory "Pappy" Boyington received the Medal of Honor and the Navy Cross. His 1958 autobiography, *Baa Baa Black Sheep*, was used as the basis for the TV series that ran for a couple of years in the seventies.

Boyington, a heavy smoker, died of lung cancer in 1988 at age 75.

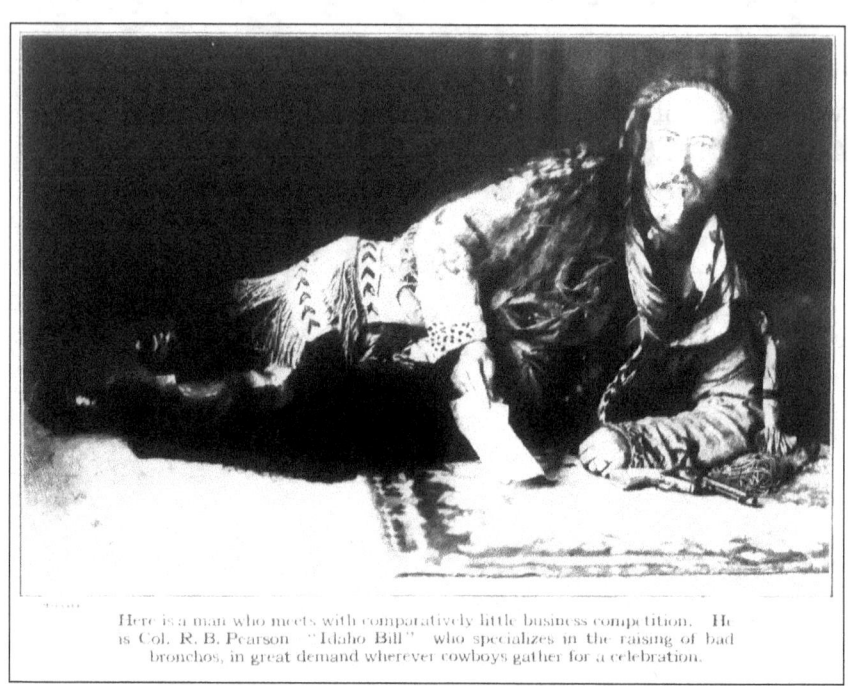

Idaho Bill as seen in Frank Leslie's Weekly, *Christmas issue, 1920.*

IDAHO BILL

Idaho Bill was a well-known character in the 1920s. While researching him, I found a hundred or so mentions of his exploits in newspapers nationwide. One of the few states where newspapers seemed to ignore him was Idaho.

When Idaho searches turned up scant evidence of Idaho Bill, I began to wonder if his nickname had anything to do with Idaho at all.

I first ran across Col. R.B. Pearson—popularly known as Idaho Bill—in a *Leslie's Weekly* from September 1921. The gist of the article was that the Colonel was providing a service to rodeos that had recently become a necessity. Rodeos had previously found unbroken horses at about any cattle ranch nearby. But in the 1920s, ranches could no longer afford to keep horses that weren't ready to work. So, Idaho Bill and some other entrepreneurs began gathering up broncos with bad reputations to supply to rodeos. For $600 to $1000, he would supply rodeos with 25 or 30 horses for three or four days, guaranteeing that they would buck.

The Leslie's article, and many others I found, said that Col. R.B. Pearson was born—probably without the rank—at or near Hastings, Nebraska, while his folks were coming west on the Oregon Trail. That story morphed around a bit, but the upshot was that he was not born in Idaho. I found a reliable source that said he was also not born on the Oregon Trail but in Sweden. His parents came to Nebraska when he was four.

R.B. Pearson went by Barney in his early days. His Swedish name, Bonde (pronounced boon-duh) was just not American enough. His father bought a ranch in the Weiser area and asked his son to run it.

According to many newspaper articles, Idaho Bill was a favorite Indian scout for Buffalo Bill, George Armstrong Custer, and others. How a transplanted Idahoan even met those people is open to speculation. Especially when Buffalo Bill died when Idaho Bill was eight.

Idaho Bill had a habit of roping anything that moved. Cows were no challenge for him, so he began roping wolves and coyotes. In 1921, newspapers all around the country ran a story datelined El Paso that began, "A wild cinnamon bear went joy riding out San Antonio Street in a claw-torn open car. Col. R.B. Pearson, bearded invader of the wilds for the last forty-five years, was chauffeur for the bear."

The story went on to say that Idaho Bill had roped the bear as a seven-month-old cub weighing 180 pounds. Speculation was that the bear would weigh 1,100 pounds when fully grown.

"This is the ninth bear Colonel Pearson has roped." The article stated. "He handled lions in Africa by the same method."

The instinct of a carnivore when roped and dragged is probably to try to get away by pulling, so this is . . . plausible?

This wasn't the first time Idaho Bill had used his rope to impress the masses, and it wouldn't be the last. In 1908, he roped wolves and delivered them to an exhibition in Chicago. In 1927, he delivered a 375-pound cinnamon bear to President Calvin Coolidge in Washington, DC. He was said to have captured many cougars and not a few snow leopards with his lariat.

Coolidge was not the only president to be charmed by Idaho Bill. Teddy Roosevelt is said to have befriended the colonel. Some accounts say he visited Idaho Bill on a presidential tour of the state in 1903. Idaho papers covered that trip hour by hour without any mention of a side trip to Weiser.

Pearson acquired some wealth from his exploits, mostly from the wild west shows he produced. In 1923, while on his way to deliver broncos

THE IDAHO CONVERSION KIT

to a rodeo in East Las Vegas, New Mexico, Idaho Bill lost his wallet in Santa Fe. He was loading the recalcitrant horses when the wallet fell out. Idaho Bill stated that there was about $40,000 in the wallet, three $10,000 bills (yes, they were in circulation at the time), and bills of lower denomination. He was offering a reward of $20,000 for the return of his wallet. No word on whether he ever got it back.

One more story about his money might have been because of that lost wallet. In 1930, the Falls City Nebraska Journal reported that Idaho Bill kept his money in his boots. He walked around with a couple of $10,000 bills and several $1,000 bills rolled up in his boots.

Idaho Bill demonstrated his "bank" for a local congressman. He pulled out a six-gun along with the money as a deterrent to anyone who might be tempted to palm one of the bills he passed around for inspection.

A guy who walks around with $20,000 in his boots might be expected to nod enthusiastically when asked if there was money in his bronco business. A reporter for Frank Leslie's *Weekly* got this answer when he asked in 1920:

> "Not much," Idaho Bill said. "But it helps to keep alive the old spirit of the West when a man's day didn't start right unless his horse gave him a nice after-breakfast shake-up. Plain ranching is too confining these days, too much fence and too few good riders and bad horses. Then this business gives me a chance to see my old friends all over the West once a year or more, and there's some satisfaction in being welcome wherever there's a chuck wagon and a few punchers. I just naturally love a real buckin' broncho anyway, and so I manage to keep a few."

Idaho Bill, a man with solid Idaho roots, died in Los Angeles in 1942.

The grave of John Baptiste Charbonneau was recognized as a Registered National Historic Place on March 14, 1973. It is located about 100 miles southwest of Ontario, Oregon. Just follow Hwy 95 southwest of Jordan Valley about 17 miles to Danner, then two miles west of Hwy 95 at Ruby Ranch.

POMP

If you picture the dollar coin that features Sacajawea (or Sacagawea, if you prefer), you may remember the eagle on the obverse, and you might remember that Shoshone Tribal member Randy'L Teton served as the model for Sacajawea. *But did you remember that there are two people depicted on the coin?*

Jean Baptiste Charbonneau was a part of the famous trip Lewis and Clark's Corps of Discovery made to the Pacific. He would not remember the trip because he was just a baby on his mother's back, as depicted on the dollar coin. He played an important role just the same. Seeing a woman with a child as part of that strange group, which included a black man and a giant black dog, helped assure tribes they encountered that this was not a war party.

William Clark took a liking to the boy, giving him the nickname "Pomp." More than that, after the death of Sacajawea, Clark took him in and paid for his education.

Jean Baptiste spoke English and French fluently. His father was Toussaint Charbonneau, a French trader who also went along on the expedition. Pomp knew Shoshone well, thanks to his mother, and could converse in several Indian languages. During six years in Europe, he also picked up German and Spanish.

Charbonneau led expeditions in the West and guided others. In 1846, he was the head guide for the Mormon Battalion's trek from Kansas to San Diego. He was a trapper, gambler, magistrate, and freighter. He prospected for gold and once owned a hotel in northern California. He even served as mayor of Mission San Luis Rey de Francia, near San Diego, for a time.

Pomp probably died as the result of an accident at a river crossing in Oregon when he was on his way, perhaps, to the mines in the

Owyhees. His destination is uncertain as are the exact details of his death. An obituary for Jean Baptiste appeared in the *Owyhee Avalanche* in 1866, listing pneumonia as the cause of death.

There is a competing story about Jean Baptiste Charbonneau, who died on the Wind River Reservation in Wyoming in 1885. Evidence that this was the Charbonneau that accompanied Lewis and Clark is slim.

The grave of John Baptiste Charbonneau, about 100 miles southwest of Ontario, Oregon, is listed on the national register of historic places and boasts no fewer than three historic markers.

LITTLE JO

Have you ever fantasized about starting a new life? Perhaps no one ever did that more completely than Little Jo Monaghan. Jo showed up in Ruby City, Idaho Territory, in 1867 or 1868, determined to try his hand at mining. He was a slight little guy, no more than five feet tall, but he was a real worker. He dug with the best of them for several weeks, then decided mining was just too tough.

Jo Monaghan then became a sheepherder, spending three years mostly in the company of sheep. After that, he worked in a livery for a time and took to breaking horses for a living. He was so good at it that Andrew Whalen hired him to work in Whalen's Wild West Show, billing the bronc rider as Cowboy Joe. Whalen offered $25 to anyone who could find a horse the man couldn't ride.

Eventually, Jo homesteaded near Rockville, Idaho. He built a cabin and raised a few livestock, living a quiet life. He served on juries and voted in elections. Jo Monaghan was a respected member of the community. A quiet man. Except that he wasn't.

In 1904, Jo Monaghan passed away. The Weiser Signal marked Jo's death with the headline, "Sex is Discovered After Death," and noted that, "There are a number of people residing in Weiser, who knew the supposed man intimately, and never had a suspicion that she was not what she represented to be."

Jo Monaghan was a woman. Who that woman was is still open to speculation. One story often told is that she was from a wealthy New York family and had found herself in a family way. As that story goes, she left her child for her sister to raise and headed West. It wasn't uncommon for women at that time to travel as men to help assure their safety. Jo may have done that and simply found it convenient to keep up the ruse.

The story has fascinated people for decades. A 1993 movie called *The Ballad of Little Joe*, written and directed by Maggie Greenwald and starring Suzy Amis as Jo, told a version of her life.

The part of the story that always interested me was that he voted. No, make that SHE voted. She might have been one of the first women to cast a vote in the United States.

HAVING TEA WITH LADY BLUEBIRD

Most of the stories in this section are Idaho-related facts about famous people. Infamy was more Lyda Southard's cup of tea. *Don't drink that tea!* Southard, who had more names than a centipede has feet, caught one she didn't seek: Lady Bluebeard.

The country's first widely known female serial killer, Lyda, wasn't born in Idaho. Her birthplace—in 1892—was a little town in Missouri. Her family moved to the Twin Falls area when she was a teenager.

Though she came from a poor family, Lyda found a way to make a good living. She worked in insurance.

Lyda collected husbands. She married Robert Dooley in 1912. They lived with Robert's bachelor brother, Ed, on a farm near Twin Falls. The Dooleys had a daughter, Loraine (some accounts say Laura), in 1914.

In 1915, Lyda collected insurance money after the tragic deaths of her first husband, Robert, their daughter, and Robert's brother, Ed. The deaths were chalked up to dirty well water, typhoid fever, and ptomaine poisoning, respectively.

Lyda was a looker, by some accounts. *Her prison photo may not reflect that, but who looks good in their mugshot?* She used her charms to marry another man in 1917, William G. McHaffie. McHaffie had a three-year-old daughter, but not for long. The daughter died shortly after they married. The newlyweds moved to Montana, where, in 1918, Mr. McHaffie, doubly unlucky, died of influenza and diphtheria. Lyda, always practical, collected the insurance money.

Then she got married again. She waited a respectful nearly five months before hitching to Harlan C. Lewis, an automobile salesman from Billings. Lewis lasted four months. He died from complications related to gastroenteritis.

It was just over a year before Lyda found her fourth husband, Edward F. Meyer, a ranch foreman from Twin Falls. Tragedy struck again, this time just a few weeks after the marriage when Meyer died from typhoid. He did not go easily. A nurse noted how concerned Lyda was about his health and that she always seemed to be giving him sips of water. Alas, the water didn't save him. The insurance payout this time was $12,000.

The coincidences surrounding this woman so unlucky in love began to raise the suspicions of Twin Falls chemist Earl Dooley. The Dooley name was not a coincidence. The chemist was a relative of Lyda's first husband. He pressed for an investigation. Said investigation found evidence of arsenic poisoning in the bodies of Lyda's hapless husbands and in the cookware she had regularly used. They also found a large supply of flypaper in the basement of a house where she had lived. Flypaper at that time was coated with arsenic.

Meanwhile, Lyda wasn't sitting still. A few weeks after Meyer's death, she snagged Paul Southard. The Navy man resisted her insistence on buying life insurance, telling her the Navy would provide for her in the event of his death.

The happy couple was living in Honolulu when police came knocking. Paul Southard insisted that Lyda, his love, was innocent. After all, he'd known her well for several weeks.

When newspapers got wind of the charges against Lyda, they generated headlines about the "temptress," the "Black Widow," and the "Lady Bluebeard." They followed every word in her seven-week trial.

The evidence against Lyda was circumstantial, but there was a ton of it. The jury was reluctant to sentence a pretty 29-year-old woman to death. They convicted her of second-degree murder. She got ten years.

THE IDAHO CONVERSION KIT

Ten years in prison kept Lyda off the husband track. Mostly. In 1931, she escaped with a prison trusty, David Minton, who had been released two weeks earlier. Lyda climbed out of her cell courtesy of a handmade rope and a rose trellis.

Authorities found Minton a few months later in Denver. He denied any connection to Lyda, but they soon picked up the trail. She was also in Denver, working as a housekeeper. She already had her clutches on a new man, Harry Whitlock. He was a bit more cautious than Lyda's previous husbands. Whitlock flatly refused to let her take out a $20,000 insurance policy on him. He wasn't surprised when the police showed up. Lyda, meanwhile, had skipped town.

Police caught up with Lyda in Kansas 15 months after her escape. She went back to prison in Idaho for another ten years. Lyda was released in 1941 and pardoned in 1943.

Lyda's movements after her release are a little sketchy. Eventually, she moved to Provo, Utah, and started a second-hand store. She also started her seventh marriage to a man named Hal Shaw. Shaw's adult children found out who Lyda was. A divorce soon followed.

Lyda Shaw was the name chiseled onto her headstone in the Twin Falls cemetery. She had the last names of Trueblood, Dooley, McHaffie, Lewis, Meyer, Southard, and Whitlock. She's most often remembered as Lyda Southard since that's the name she was using when she first entered prison. Lyda was sometimes Lydia on official records. Whatever you call her, she earned the title of murderess.

LADY MANN

Cynthia Mann arrived in Boise an invalid in June 1879. Her journey across southern Idaho, lying on a pallet on the floor of a stagecoach, had been so brutal that at one point she begged to be left at a stage station so she could die beneath a roof.

Born in Kentucky and educated in Kansas, Cynthia Mann began teaching when she was just 18 years old. At age 26, her husband, Samuel Mann, whom she would later divorce, brought her to Boise with the hope that the change of climate might improve her health. Something did, for she became a dynamo in local affairs related to education, suffrage, politics, and prohibition.

Mann taught at several schools in Boise and in nearby communities. She was often mentioned in early papers as a teacher at Cloverdale, Cole, Central School, and Park School. She was one of the organizers of the Idaho State Teachers Association, and in 1906 ran for Superintendent of Public Schools on the Prohibitionist ticket.

"Lady Mann" was the affectionate nickname given to her by students, who were intensely loyal to her. She taught hundreds of children, and the children of those children, through the years. She is best remembered as the teacher of the "ungraded" school at the Children's Home Finding and Aid Society of Idaho. That organization began in 1908 as a residence and adoption center for homeless children. It exists today as the Children's Home Society of Idaho, carrying on its mission of placing children in good homes, though it is no longer a residence institution.

The handsome stone building, designed by Tourtellotte and Company, for the Children's Home Finding and Aid Society of Idaho is located at 740 E. Warm Springs Avenue. It is so located because of Cynthia Mann. Never a wealthy woman, Mann was savvy about real estate and owned a fair amount of it. She donated almost

THE IDAHO CONVERSION KIT

Cynthia Mann was one of Idaho's best-known philanthropists. This photo was taken of her when she was Cynthia Pease, age 16, in Lawrence, Kansas. Photo courtesy Idaho State Historical Society.

the entire block where the Society is located today, then went on to make many more donations large and small over the years.

Cynthia Mann was sometimes called a "club woman." She tirelessly supported education and political reform as one of the early members of the Columbian Club and a founding member of the Boise chapter of the Daughters of the American Revolution. She was active in the YWCA, the Business Women's Club, and the Council of Women Voters.

Man spoke often on the history of suffrage in Idaho and went to Washington, DC more than once to lobby for national women's suffrage. It was on a trip to DC to visit her brother in 1911 when she almost met her end.

Mrs. Mann was reading the inscription on a "Peace Monument," erected in memory of soldiers and sailors when a woman driving a horse and buggy knocked her down and ran over her. Bleeding from severe facial injuries and dazed, she was taken to a local Casualty hospital that had a shady reputation.

As she told the story, "I was badly cut about the face, in two places on my lip, sustained a bad gash in my forehead, and my feet were bruised. My head was bothering me more than any other portion of my anatomy, and it was just 24 hours after I begged for it that I got any ice to put on it, and this in the face of the terrible summer heat."

To her good fortune, Addison T. Smith, secretary to Senator Weldon B. Heyburn of Idaho, read about her accident in the newspaper. "Mr. Smith came for me at once and insisted on taking me to his home and I feel that I owe my life to him and Mrs. Smith."

The *Idaho Statesman*, in reporting about the incident, called Cynthia Mann "perhaps the greatest philanthropist in the state of Idaho."

To, as they say, add insult to injury, Mann was robbed by a nurse while in the hospital. She got her $20 back only after Smith and a Congressman French put pressure on the institution.

Cynthia Mann continued her activism and her teaching until February 1920. She qualified for a small pension, but at age 66 refused to quit teaching. Her health was starting to fail, so she got her affairs in order, which in her case meant creating a will that gave her remaining funds to her beloved clubs, for hospital work in South America, and $800 for the rehabilitation of a small village, Tilliloy, in northern France. She left most of the money for the construction of the Ward Massacre site monument to the Pioneer Chapter of the D.A.R.

THE IDAHO CONVERSION KIT

On February 6, 1920, Cynthia Mann died of pneumonia following a bout of influenza.

Lady Mann planned her own funeral to the last detail. The following is a portion of what was read at the service, at her request.

"I had a dream which was not all a dream. I dreamed I was the children's friend, that I loved them enough to give them pain, if by so doing, they might grow up good and true and beautiful in the sight of God. I loved them enough to go without what was unnecessary that they might have what would put good things into their lives: sweet thoughts and beautiful memories."

Also at her request, Cynthia Mann's body was carried by a group of her early pupils to be put to rest in Morris Hill Cemetery. Her marker reads, "It was Happiness to Serve."

Advertisement for The Ramblin' Kid, *a novel by Earl Wayland Bowman.*

THE RAMBLIN' KID

Agnes Just Reid, a well-known regional writer, and my great aunt, corresponded with several Western writers in her day, including B.M. Bower and Frank Robertson. One of Bower's books, *Ranch of the Wolverine*, was written while she was staying with Agnes.

The family has some correspondence and other clues and scraps about another writer she was friends with. He went by the nickname "The Ramblin' Kid." In his correspondence, he would sometimes refer to Agnes as "The Range Cayuse," after a book of poetry she wrote of the same name. *The Ramblin' Kid* was a successful novel by the author, whose real name was Earl Wayland Bowman.

When I did the requisite digging, I found his Idaho roots run deep, though he was born in Missouri in 1875. Orphaned at about age ten, he spent many years knocking around Texas and the Southwest working any cowboy kind of job that came his way. This early experience would serve him well as a writer of the American West.

Somewhere along the line, he learned how to set type and made his living as a traveling printer. It seemed only natural that he would come up with something to print.

He and his wife, Elva, moved to Idaho in 1901, living first in Weiser, then on a ranch he built up near Council. He began writing for several local papers, everything from letters to the editor to poetry. The latter was dense with a religious slant but apparently popular with readers. He wrote poems regularly for the *Idaho Statesman* for several years.

Bowman started a periodical titled *Homeseekers Monthly*, essentially a real estate rag. It later morphed into a magazine called *The Golden Trail*. It featured short stories, poetry, and articles about Idaho written by Bowman and other writers. It was in *The Golden Trail* that he began developing his persona as "The Ramblin' Kid."

A frequent orator at political gatherings of the day, Bowman somehow got himself elected as an Idaho State Senator in 1914. I'm not the only one who finds this startling. "The Ramblin' Kid" was a socialist and the only state senator of that persuasion ever elected in Idaho. He got several bills through the Legislature, including the Emergency Employment Act, which put the burden on counties to create jobs for everyone who needed one. Counties heartily resisted it. The Idaho Supreme Court found it unconstitutional 18 months later. Bowman lost the next election and went back to writing.

He passed away in southern California in 1952. His family donated Bowman's papers to Boise State College in 1972.

Among those papers was a 1923 letter to Agnes Just Reid in which he groused about correspondence he had received from the California State Librarian who wanted biographical information on him as a California author. He replied that he was "an Idaho author if any kind," and added to Agnes, "I'm all Idaho and want to stay that way."

"PAPA" HEMINGWAY

Idaho has more than its fair share of well-known native writers, from Pulitzer Prize Winner Marilyn Robinson to Laurel Thatcher Ulrich, who is remembered for the line, "Well-behaved women seldom make history."

Perhaps the best-known writer associated with the state is Ernest Hemingway. But call him "Papa." Hemingway hated his first name. He began encouraging friends to call him "Papa" when he was in his twenties.

"Papa" Hemingway discovered Idaho in 1939. Averell Harriman, then the President of Union Pacific Railroad, invited Hemingway and a slew of Hollywood celebrities to visit Sun Valley Lodge. Harriman built the ski area, the country's first destination resort, to attract tourists who would purchase train tickets.

Celebrities came and went, assuring a measure of fame for the ski resort. Hemingway developed a deep love for the place. His passion for hunting and fishing played out in and around the Wood River Valley for years.

In 1958, Fidel Castro came to power. Castro confiscated Hemingway's beloved home in Cuba. In 1960, "Papa" left Cuba for the last time.

Hemingway was having trouble with his writing, finding it difficult to stay on track. His eyesight was failing, and he was becoming paranoid, disorganized, and confused. Rumors had him on his deathbed. His wife, Mary, moved him to Ketchum, where they had bought a house the year before, to get him out of the public eye and give him a chance for recuperation.

While living in Sun Valley, Hemingway worked on parts of *For Whom the Bell Tolls*, *Islands in the Stream*, *The Garden of Eden*, and *A Moveable Feast*.

After moving permanently to Idaho, Hemingway spent some time at the Mayo Clinic under an assumed name. His treatment there included many rounds of electroshock therapy. Further treatment had little positive effect. "Papa" Hemingway took his own life with his favorite shotgun on July 2, 1961.

Hemingway is buried in the Ketchum Cemetery. A monument to the writer is located off Trail Creek Road in Sun Valley. The inscription on the monument is from a eulogy he wrote for a close friend, Gene Van Guilder. It reads:

> "He loved the warm sun of summer and the high mountain meadows, the trails through the timber, and the sudden clear blue of the lakes. He loved the hills in the winter when the snow comes. Best of all he loved the fall . . . the fall with the tawny and grey, the leaves yellow on the cottonwoods, leaves floating on the trout streams and above the hills the high blue windless skies. He loved to shoot, he loved to ride, and he loved to fish."

Ernest Hemingway and his cat, Boise, outside his home, Finca Vigia, in Cuba. Photo courtesy Ernest Hemingway Photographs Collection, John F. Kennedy Presidential Library and Museum, Boston.

STEP 8
THE JOCKEY BOX

The Idaho "Jockey Box," a place for gloves, a map or two, and . . . a hatchet?

THE JOCKEY BOX

What comes to mind when you hear the term "jockey box"? If you've been around Idaho for a while, you probably think of what most people in the U.S. call a "glove compartment." If you're new to the state, you're likely baffled by the term.

Knowing that it was a mystery to a lot of folks, I did a little research. I found the first instance of the term in an October 18, 1881 edition of the *Idaho World,* an Idaho City paper. It was mentioned during an interview with convicted murderer Henry McDonald. In describing the murder of George Meyer, McDonald said, "He and I then got into a quarrel about the dog, and he came at me, I pushed him, and he fell over a sagebrush; he got up and started for the jockey box to get a six-shooter…" The jockey box, in that instance, was probably a box beneath the seat of the man's wagon or buckboard.

The next mention of the phrase is from the *Idaho Daily Statesman,* June 23, 1896. A couple of lines tell the story, "He opened the jockey box on his seat and rummaged around in it, finally producing a small hatchet and a big nail.

"'I guess you'll have to drive her out with this,' said he, and he sat down on the ground and hung on to a buckeye bush with both hands while one of his companions placed the end of the nail against the side of the tooth and hit it with the hatchet."

Cowboy dentistry.

Note that those early mentions were about wagons, not cars. The term referred to a small (as jockeys are supposed to be) box in which one stored certain essentials, such as guns and dental tools. That small box inside automobiles that served the same purpose picked up the same name in Idaho and other Western states.

So, laugh all you want, but what do you store in YOUR glove box? Gloves? Maybe.

More likely the owner's manual, an old CD, your registration, a couple of pens that don't work, 16 cents, and a four-year-old peppermint.

So, why call it a glove compartment? Jockey box is a nice, generic term to indicate that the box is equivalent to the junk drawer in your house. You know, a place to put your hatchet.

STEP 9
THE GEM STATE

Graphite and cut diamond. Photos courtesy Wikipedia: graphite by Robert M. Lavinsky and diamond by Amcyrus2012.

THE GEM STATE

If you haven't already learned it, you soon will. Idaho's nickname is "The Gem State." *See what you just learned?* The next logical question is, *why?* Sorry, there's no definitive answer to that one, but it's probably because of the abundance of minerals and gems in Idaho, from silver and lead to precious and semi-precious stones.

The rarest is our state gemstone, the star garnet. Suffice it to say garnets aren't especially rare, but star garnets are. They are found only in Idaho and India. We have more arms on our stars than those in India, though. You can find four-star garnets in both places, but only Idaho has six-star garnets.

Just about every stone you can think of has been found in Idaho at one time or another, including diamonds. You won't get rich searching for diamonds in Idaho, though one of our territorial governors tried making himself rich convincing Idahoans there were plenty of diamonds. Caleb Lyon, the second governor of Idaho Territory, famously embezzled more than $46,000 intended for the Boise Shoshoni Tribe while he was in office. It's less well-known that he started a frenzy of diamond prospecting by claiming that a diamond had been found near Ruby City. Hundreds flocked to stake their claims. Not a single diamond was found. However, the largest diamond ever found in the United States did show up in Idaho. The nineteen-and-a-half-carat diamond turned up somewhere between New Meadows and McCall.

Our neighboring states, Montana and Wyoming, have vast coal reserves. Idaho has a few veins that were commercially mined for a few years, but nothing to brag about. *And why did I bring up coal?* It's almost a gem. A pre-diamond, if you will.

STEP 10
FAMOUS CONNECTIONS

Boise has two statues of President Abraham Lincoln. The first is on the capitol grounds in front of the Idaho Statehouse. It is the oldest Lincoln statue in the West.

The statue was first installed at the Soldiers Home in 1915, then moved to the Idaho Veterans Home in East Boise. In 2009 it was moved to its present location. It's one of six duplicates of a piece sculpted by Alphonso Pelzer.
The original statue is in New Jersey.

The other Lincoln is a giant sculpture, 9 feet tall, and he's sitting on a bench. You can sit with him in Julia Davis Park. The Lincoln sculpture is a copy of one created by Gutzon Borglum, who also carved the faces on Mount Rushmore.
He was born in St. Charles, Idaho Territory, in 1867.
The original sitting Lincoln is also in New Jersey.

Why two Lincolns in Idaho?
Lincoln signed the act creating Idaho Territory in 1863.

From Speaking of Idaho history posts by Rick Just, https://www.rickjust.com

ABRAHAM LINCOLN NEVER SLEPT HERE

Abraham Lincoln never slept here, but Idaho has a ton of connections to Lincoln. So many that they have become an obsession for Lincoln scholar and former Idaho Attorney General David Leroy.

Leroy has spent a lifetime collecting Lincoln memorabilia and documenting his connections with Idaho. The most visible result of his passion is the exhibit *Abraham Lincoln, His Legacy in Idaho* at the Idaho State Historical Society Archives. Donated by David and Nancy Leroy in 2010, the exceptional exhibit displays more than 200 documents and artifacts.

So, what are the connections? Lincoln personally lobbied Congress for the creation of Idaho Territory and signed that creation into law on March 3, 1863. But his interest in what would become our state started much earlier. Lincoln sought to be Idaho's governor. Well, not exactly, but he did seek to govern Oregon Territory in 1849, part of which would one day become Idaho.

Lincoln was there at a meeting where it was decided the name of the new territory would be Idaho.

Many of the Lincoln connections were by way of Illinois and Indiana. His friends and neighbors helped shape the state. Samuel C. Parks, a law partner, was the territory's first associate Supreme Court Justice. Another friend was Idaho's seventh territorial governor, Mason Brayman. Lincoln's bodyguard, Ward Hill Lamon, sought appointment as a territorial governor of Idaho from Lincoln's successor, Andrew Johnson, but he did not get it.

Years after Lincoln's death, a childhood playmate of Lincoln's sons became the U.S. Marshall of Idaho Territory, then a territorial congressional delegate. Fred T. Dubois lobbied hard to create the State of Idaho and to keep it from being split off and claimed by its neighbors.

On the day of Lincoln's death, April 14, 1865, he had a meeting with Idaho's delegate, William H. Wallace, about filling an Idaho supreme court vacancy. Wallace was said to have been invited to see a play that night with the Lincolns. He declined.

There's a terrific little book about Lincoln's connections to Idaho called *Lincoln Never Slept Here, Idaho's Abraham Lincoln Bicentennial Tour* written by Todd Shallat, Ph.D., with Kathleen Craven Tuck.

DANIEL BOONE

Daniel Boone was a celebrated frontiersman back when the frontier included parts of Pennsylvania, North Carolina, and Kentucky. He first gained fame during the American Revolution when he and a group of men recaptured three girls, one was Boone's daughter, from an Indian war party recruited by the British. James Fenimore Cooper wrote a fictionalized version of the event in *Last of the Mohicans*.

That was in 1776. *Why do we in Idaho care?* Because his well-documented exploits at that time seem to have placed him some 1,800 miles away from Idaho, not somewhere on the Continental Divide, carving his misspelled name into an aspen tree.

In 1976, an Idaho Falls woman named Louise Rutledge became intrigued by an inscription on an aspen tree that said, "D. Boon 1776." The carving was old. Well, maybe not 1776 old, but certainly not as new as 1976. Rutledge wrote a little book called *D. Boon 1776 A Western Bicentennial Mystery*. According to the Sunday, August 10, 1976, edition of the *Idaho Statesman*, she "began extensive research to prove—or disprove—that frontiersman Daniel Boone was, in fact, in Idaho 30 years ahead of Lewis and Clark."

Rutledge became convinced that Boone had carved his initials into the tree, not in spite of, but because of the absence of the "e" at the end of his name. She had grown up in the Cumberland Gap area of Tennessee, which was awash in tales about "Boon trees." She was certain that because of the misspelling, this carving was genuine. Many "Boon trees" were scattered around the south, often with the added information that D. Boon had "cilled or kilt or killed a bar"—"bar" being the way a genuine frontiersman would spell "bear." We can't know how many or if any of those carvings are genuine, but we know that Daniel Boone always knew how to spell it when signing or printing his name.

Not ready to leave a good story untold, Rutledge, her husband, Gene, and Bonita Pendleton, all of Idaho Falls, wrote a play speculating on Boone's journey to Idaho called *D. Boone 1776, War Has Two Sides*.

Tree experts later determined that the Idaho aspen carving was done in about 1895. Undeterred, Rutledge postulated that someone had seen the original, genuine D. Boon tree and noticed that it was dead. To preserve history for posterity, they made a copy.

Well, it's a theory.

News clipping featuring Bonita Pendleton and Gene Rutledge from the Post Register, *August 3, 1976.*

DAVID LYNCH

W*hat do* Eraserhead, Elephant Man, *and Monroe Elementary School have in common?* They all have connections to director David Lynch. Lynch, born in Missoula, spent several years in Boise when his dad was working for the US Department of Agriculture as a researcher in the 1950s. He attended both Monroe Elementary and South Junior High. His father's job also took the family to Sandpoint for a while.

Lynch's more famous movies also include *Blue Velvet, Mulholland Drive,* and *Dune,* though the latter was a bit of a flop. TV audiences know him best as the creator of *Twin Peaks.*

In Boise, Lynch was a little notorious for his bombs. Not the box office kind. He's quoted on the *City of Absurdity* website as saying, "We were all, um, heavily into making bombs at that particular place and time." He built one rocket out of match heads and was tamping them down when it went off, sending the rocket through his ankle. They "sewed[my] foot back on and [I] was okay after that."

Until the next bombing, "We blew up a swimming pool. I was arrested." He went on to say, "We didn't blow it up; we set off a bomb in there—actually for safety reasons. The pool was built off the ground. These bombs we were making were pipe bombs, and they would hit the ground and not explode until they were about eye level. And they would explode with such a force that the pipe would just completely turn inside out, and shrapnel would blow.

Publicity photo of David Lynch, American filmmaker, visual artist, musician and actor.

We threw it in the pool so that the shrapnel would hit the side of the pool. We threw it in around ten o'clock Saturday morning, and the smoke came up shaped like the pool. This thing rose just instantly, shaped like the pool. Just for a moment, till the wind blew it. It filled the pool with smoke, and it just took that shape. And you could hear it for, I don't know how far, but it shook windows supposedly for five blocks. It was a big bomb."

I did a little search for that incident in the *Idaho Statesman* with no success. I did find Lynch attending a swimming birthday party for a classmate, on the ski lift at Bogus, playing a brass instrument in a summer music program at South Junior High, elected as seventh-grade president at South, on a dance committee, in a play, and earning a merit badge.

So, clearly, he was on the road to fame.

JIMMY STEWART

The burning question in Boise on Valentine's Day, 1943, was *"Is Jimmy Stewart really here?"* The *Idaho Statesman* that day reported in its "About Town" column that it was a rumor. "But that didn't prevent Boise's female population from dreaming, wondering, anticipating—and taking a good second look at every lieutenant they passed on the street."

On page one of the same edition, the story read, "He's Jimmy Stewart to millions of movie fans, but at Gowen Field Saturday he registered as First Lt. James M. Stewart, and on the routine registration forms, in the listing his occupation in civilian life he placed a question mark after the word 'actor.'"

Stewart had been determined to serve his country. When he tried to enlist in the army, they turned him down because he was too skinny. At six-foot-three, he tipped the scale at only 138 pounds. So, putting on weight became his goal. He started on a diet heavy with steaks, pasta, and milkshakes. When he stepped on the scales at his second physical in March 1941, he was still a little shy of the minimum weight, but someone fudged the figures by a few ounces, and Jimmy Stewart was on his way to boot camp.

Eager as he was to serve, it was a bit of an adjustment. He'd been averaging $12,000 a week as an actor, according to the article "Mr. Stewart Goes to War," by Richard L. Hayes on the *HistoryNet* website. An army private's pay was $21 a month. It is reported that he sent $2.10 a month to his agent.

Stewart had a college degree from Princeton, and he was already licensed to fly multi-engine planes, so it was no surprise when he got his commission in January 1942. That meant he could wear his uniform when he presented Gary Cooper with the Academy Award for best actor for Cooper's performance in Sergeant York. Stewart had won the Oscar the year before for his role in *Philadelphia Story*.

The actor became a flight instructor, serving first at Mather Field, California, then transferred to Kirkland, New Mexico for bombardier school. He was at another base in New Mexico and HQ for the Second Air Force in Salt Lake City before coming to Boise, where he was a flight instructor for B-17s. He was also a sensation.

The "About Town" column on February 21, 1943, read, "Being constantly on the lookout for Jimmy Stewart has made Boiseans celebrity-conscious. We could have sworn we've been seeing Lucille Ball and John Garfield night-spotting about town . . . but it turned out to be Eileen Cummock, beauteous Gowen Field civilian employee, and Capt. Cox."

"About Town" was breathless with chatter about Stewart. It wasn't until June 21 that the paper published an actual photograph of the "ordinary American serving his country." He was shown visiting backstage at a Gowen Field minstrel show at the Pinney Theater. They published another six days later of Stewart shaking hands with someone at a "recent Gowen Field Frolic."

In July of that year, Stewart got his captain's bars and was called back to Hollywood to attend a wedding. In August, his stint in Boise was over. His stint in the military had just begun.

Jimmy Stewart would fly twenty bombing missions over Europe in World War II. Those were the missions he was credited with. He often flew self-assigned as a combat crewman when he was a commander. Oddly, he flew on one bombing mission in Vietnam as a non-duty observer in a B-52 when he was Air Force Reserve Brigadier General Stewart in 1966. He retired from the Air Force in 1968. In 1985, President Reagan promoted him to Major

General on the retired list and presented him with the Presidential Medal of Freedom.

Stewart didn't spend a lot of time talking about the war or his military service. In fact, his movie contracts always included a clause that his military service would not be used as part of the publicity for the movie. Stewart passed away in 1997.

President Ronald Reagan presented Jimmy Stewart with the Presidential Medal of Freedom in 1985.

KING OF THE ROAD

There seems to be one indisputable fact about Roger Miller's hit "King of the Road." He wrote it. *But where did he write it?* That this would even be a question of interest is somewhat puzzling. Sure, it was a big hit. But why would people argue about its provenance?

Miller's concert chat seems to have been the reason for the confusion. He would often toss out a line about where he wrote the song or where he first saw the sign that became the first line, "Trailers for sale or rent." He mentioned seeing it in Chicago, Kitchener, Ontario, and Indiana. He bought a little statue of a hobo someplace that is said to have inspired him. One of those places was the Boise airport.

Miller often said from the stage that the song was written in Boise, Idaho. I like that version because I heard it first from a man who claimed to have been there when it was written.

Bob Weisenberger was the manager of KGEM radio in Boise, where I worked for about six years. He told of sitting in a hotel room listening to Roger Miller jam with Boxcar Willie following Miller's performance at the Snake River Stampede in Nampa. Boxcar Willie became a concert draw himself over the following couple of decades, and he even had a minor hit with a cover of "King of the Road." At the time this took place, probably 1964, Boxcar Willie was a DJ at KGEM, using the name Marty Martin.

Many reports about the genesis of "King of the Road" say it was written at the Idanha. It's such an iconic Boise hotel that those reports just seem right. Maybe not. Miller himself reminded the crowd gathered for a press conference in 1972 to promote another appearance at the Snake River Stampede that he had written the song while staying at the Hotel Boise, room 607, which today is one of the rooms in Congressman Mike Simpson's Boise office.

Wherever he wrote it—and it was probably written over a period of at least weeks, perhaps coming together finally in Boise—Miller would never need to work "two hours of pushin' broom" for his accommodations after its release. The song won 1965 Grammy awards for Best Contemporary Rock 'N Roll Single, Best Contemporary Vocal Performance, Best Country & Western Recording, Best Country Vocal Performance, and Best Country Song.

Roger Miller told countless stories about how his song, "King of the Rad," came about.

Julia Jean "Judy" Turner was born in Wallace, Idaho. She later was known as Lana Turner.

LANA TURNER

On February 8, 1921, Mildred Turner was four days shy of her 17th birthday when she gave birth to a girl, Julia Jean, in Wallace, Idaho. John and Mildred Turner lived up a narrow canyon in the mining town of Burke at the time. In 1925, the small family moved to Wallace. John Turner, who had been a mine inspector, opened a dry-cleaning establishment there and worked part-time in the nearby silver mines.

The Turners called their daughter Judy. She showed an interest in performing when she was three, doing some dance routines at various events.

When Judy was six, the Turners moved to San Francisco, separating shortly after. It was there in 1930 that tragedy struck. John Turner won a little money in a craps game. He stuffed his winnings in his sock and headed home. He never got there. Authorities found him bludgeoned to death, his left shoe and sock missing. The murder was never solved.

Judy Turner is not remembered for the dreadful story of her father's death. She is remembered as THAT girl. Her story is so well-worn as a Hollywood legend that it seems mythical. She was spotted at the Top Hat Malt Shop on Sunset Boulevard sipping a Coke while skipping a typing class at Hollywood High. The publisher of the *Hollywood Reporter* did the spotting. He asked her if she was interested in being in the movies. Her famous answer was, "I'll have to ask my mother first."

Mom said yes, and the reporter sent her to see Zeppo Marx, the youngest of the Marx brothers, who was a talent agent, as well as an actor.

Somewhere along the line, Judy became Lana Turner. She had a four-decade career in film, appearing in 56 movies, including *Peyton Place* in 1958, for which she received an Academy Award nomination for Best Actress in a Leading Role.

There was a stormy chapter in her life that received much press at the time. She was dating reputed mobster Johnny Stompanato. The relationship was tempestuous and filled with violent arguments. Stompanato confronted her with a gun on the set of *Another Time, Another Place*, which was filming in London. Co-star Sean Connery twisted the gun away from him and he ran off.

But that didn't end the off-again on-again relationship. On March 26, 1958, Turner went to the Oscar ceremony where she was contending for Best Actress. Stompanato was angry that he didn't get to go with her. He confronted Turner in her home, threatening to kill her mother and daughter. Fearing that her mother was in danger, daughter Cheryl entered the bedroom and stabbed Stompanato with a kitchen knife, killing him. National and local media covered the trial heavily. The jury found that it was a justifiable homicide.

Lana Turner, born in Idaho, died of cancer in 1974 in Los Angeles.

MICKEY MOUSE

Idaho celebrated its 100th birthday in 1990. Mickey Mouse celebrated his 60th about the same time. And, yes, there is a connection.

Lillian Marie Bounds was born in Spalding and grew up in Lapwai. She attended elementary school there, then later moved to Lewiston. She got her big break when she moved to Hollywood. Miss Bounds was "discovered" there by Walt Disney, but not in the usual sense of the word. She did not become a star at Disney Studios, where she worked as a secretary and an illustrator. She became Walt Disney's wife.

Walt Disney and Lillian Marie Bounds were married in Lewiston, Idaho July 13, 1925. That was just about when Disney created his most famous character, Mickey Mouse. He had planned to call the rodent Mortimer Mouse. His Idaho wife changed his mind, and he changed the name to . . . Mickey. From humble beginnings in a converted California garage, Mickey Mouse created an entertainment empire for the Disneys.

Lillian Disney never forgot her Idaho roots. She was well known for her philanthropy in her hometown of Lapwai, a mostly Nez Perce community, where she played high school basketball. She was an important part of Idaho entertainment. Mrs. Disney and her two daughters, Sharon and Diane, owned Retlaw Enterprises, which at one time included KLEW-TV in Lewiston, KIDK-TV in Idaho Falls, and nine other television stations out of state. Retlaw, by the way, is Walter spelled backward. A tip of the hat to the man who invented the mouse from the lady who named the mouse Mickey.

Lillian Bounds Disney, 1951. Wikipedia image, https://en.wikipedia.org/wiki/Lillian_Disney#/media/File:LilianBounds1951.jpg

PAUL BUNYAN

So, did you know that Paul Bunyan has an Idaho connection? Stories about Paul Bunyan and his giant blue ox, Babe, circulated lumber camps across the country for decades before anyone thought to write them down and publish them. Eventually, many people did. One of the best-remembered tellers of those tales was author James Stevens, who spent much of his childhood in Idaho. Sinclair Lewis called Stevens "the true son of Paul Bunyan."

Stevens was a soldier in France during World War I. He did more than fight, though. He published his Paul Bunyan stories in *Stars and Stripes*. After the war, he knocked around the country as an itinerant laborer, educating himself in local libraries wherever he went.

He published poetry in the *Saturday Evening Post* and more Paul Bunyan stories in *American Mercury*. Stevens's 1945 novel *Big Jim Turner*, about an itinerant working man and poet who grew up around Knox, Idaho, (now a ghost town), has many autobiographical elements in it. His best-known work is probably his *Paul Bunyan* book, published in 1925 by Garden City Publishing in New York. Artist Allen Lewis did the woodcut illustrations for the book. Stevens died in Seattle in 1971.

PAUL REVERE

Henry Wadsworth Longfellow should probably get top billing when you Google "Legend of Paul Revere." Sorry, Hank, Google thinks most people will be looking for the B side of a record called *Him or Me—What's It Gonna Be.*

Nowadays, that legend is about a Caldwell burger flipper who made it big as the "Madman of Rock and Roll."

Paul was going to make it big somewhere. As a teenager, he ran three barber shops, and that Caldwell burger joint called Reed and Bell Drive-In (a root beer brand name, something like A&W). Seeing opportunity in rock and roll, he began promoting dances, which led to him putting together a little rock band. At first, it was all about promoting the drive-in. Then Revere, who was Paul Revere Dick at that time, decided to make a tape. He and the band recorded a few songs at a crude little studio, and Paul took the tape to Hollywood.

That first trip to Tinsel Town set a pattern that Paul Revere would follow again and again. He would often pack up copies of a new single and set out on his Harley to hit radio stations around the country to get them to play the records.

In an interview conducted by Dominic Priore for the *Sundazed* website, Paul said, "I'd see a radio tower stickin' out of a pasture somewhere, I'd just pull in there and talk fast and convince whoever's on the air to listen to my record and do a little interview and away I'd go to the next place."

In January 1971, just a year after KFXD in Nampa started playing rock full-time, Tom Scott was working the board when Paul Revere pulled up on his bike and dug out a new record. He thought maybe "Dream Room" might be a hit. Tom played that one, as well as the flip side. It was the first time "Indian Reservation" by Paul Revere and the Raiders was heard on the radio. It would not be the last. The song went platinum, becoming Paul Revere and the Raiders' only million-selling record and their only hit to make it to number one on the *Billboard* chart.

Maybe Paul Revere thought "Indian Reservation" would be the B side because it was a cover. Written by John D. Loudermilk, Marvin Rainwater released it in 1959 as "The Pale-Faced Indian." No one noticed. But in 1968 Don Fardon took the song to Number 20 on the *Billboard Hot 100*.

One can safely say that Mark Lindsay, lead singer of Paul Revere and the Raiders, was happy about the hit. "Indian Reservation" was subtitled "The Lament of the Cherokee Reservation Indian." Lindsay, who went to Wilder High School, is part Cherokee.

Oh, and about that opening line: Google it yourself.

Searches change all the time, but it's worth Googling "The Legend of Paul Revere" and the lyrics for the song.

1967 publicity photo of Paul Revere and the Raiders. The group evolved from a Caldwell High School dance band. Left to right: Paul Revere, Mike "Smitty" Smith, Phil "Fang" Volk, Mark Lindsay, and Drake Levin. Dick Clark appears in this shot, too, pretending to be a drummer.

SCROOGE

Reginald Owen was visited by three ghosts in 1938. One of them pointed a shaking, boney finger at a headstone with his name on it. Well, the name of his character, Ebenezer Scrooge. Owen's actual headstone is in Boise's Morris Hill Cemetery.

Owen was widely acclaimed for his role as Scrooge. Around Christmas, the movie is played and replayed to—forgive the pun—death. Scrooge was probably his best-remembered character, but he played many of them. Notably, he played both Sherlock Holmes and Watson several times each. The same year he played Scrooge, Owen appeared in another movie as a character named Grump. Fortunately, that didn't typecast him.

Reggie Owen's career in film began in 1911 when he appeared as Thomas Cromwell in *Henry VIII*. His last film was *Bedknobs and Broomsticks* in 1971 in which he played Major General Sir Brian Teagler. Some might recall him as Admiral Boom in *Mary Poppins*. His life on stage was at least equal to his film career, and he was a radio star as well. In the TV era, he had a part in an episode of *Maverick* with James Garner. Finally, of trivial note, Owen rented his mansion in Bel Air to the Beatles when they performed at the Hollywood Bowl, when no hotel would book them.

And Boise? Owen had just wrapped up an appearance in *A Funny Thing Happened on the Way to the Forum* in New York when he and his wife decided to visit her son from a previous marriage. Robert Haveman was a labor relations manager at Boise Cascade. The former Barbara Haveman, Owen's third wife, was a descendent of Russian nobility who had married the actor when he was 69. He spent the last three months of his life in Boise. A stroke or heart attack took him in 1972 at age 85.

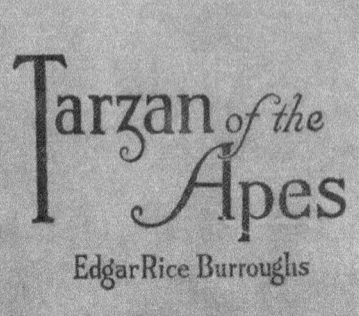

Original book cover, Tarzan of the Apes, *by Edgar Rice Burroughs, and a later illustrated color edition.*

TARZAN

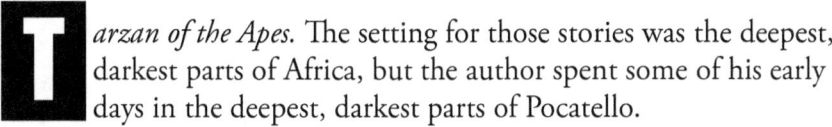

Tarzan of the Apes. The setting for those stories was the deepest, darkest parts of Africa, but the author spent some of his early days in the deepest, darkest parts of Pocatello.

Edgar Rice Burroughs came to the state in the mid-1890s. His brothers worked on a ranch their father had purchased near Yale, Idaho, (which the brothers, Yale graduates, had convinced the postal service to name), and he got a job there, too, as a cowhand. But he didn't stick with any job for very long. Burroughs worked for a local dredge company for a while, then found himself unemployed.

With the help of his brother Harry, Edgar Rice Burroughs purchased a stationery and cigar store in Pocatello at 233 West Center Street in 1898. He also established a Pocatello delivery service, sometimes delivering newspapers himself from the back of a black horse named Crow. It turned out that Burroughs was not as successful at selling books as he would later become at writing them. He sold the failing Pocatello store a year after he bought it.

He tried ranching again. He worked for a dredge company again, this time in Minidoka. He lived in the Stanley Basin for a while and even ran for office in 1904 in Parma, where he was elected alderman.

Eventually, Burroughs moved out of Idaho. His continued bouts of unemployment gave him time to try his hand at writing. In 1914, he published a book called *Tarzan of the Apes*, and its character became an international fictional hero. Edgar Rice Burroughs, a writer shaped in part by his many years in Idaho.

ABOUT THE AUTHOR

Rick Just is a native Idahoan who grew up on a ranch along the Blackfoot River. Just was born in Blackfoot, Idaho, and graduated from Firth High School. He earned a Bachelor of Arts degree in English and a Master of Public Administration from Boise State University.

Just served in the United States Marine Corps from 1969 to 1971. For 30 years, he worked for the Idaho Department of Parks and Recreation, retiring as chief planner.

Just has published four young adult novels, *The Wizards Trilogy*, consisting of *Wizard Girl* (2007), *Wizard Chase* (2012), and *Wizard's End* (2012), followed by *Ghost Writer* (2019). He also wrote *Anjel* (2014).

He has written or edited several books on Idaho history, including *100 Years: Idaho and Its Parks* (Idaho Parks and Recreation, 2008); *Idaho Snapshots* (2012); *Idaho's State Parks* (Images of America Series, 2017); and *Keeping Private Idaho* (a novel, 2018).

His most recent books are *A Kid's Guide to Boise* (2018), *Fearless: The Story of Farris Lind, the Man Behind the Skunk* (2019), and *Symbols, Signs, and Songs*, the first in the "Speaking of Idaho History" Series (2020).

Rick Just was elected to the Idaho Senate (15th District) in November 2022, and assumed office on December 1, 2022.

Published by
CEDAR CREEK PRESS, LLC
BOISE, IDAHO

www.ingramcontent.com/pod-product-compliance
Lightning Source LLC
Chambersburg PA
CBHW052141070526
44585CB00017B/1923